Vegetarian Times
Vegetarian

BEGINNER'S GUIDE

Vegetarian Times
Vegetarian
BEGINNER'S GUIDE

By the Editors of Vegetarian Times

Macmillan • USA

MACMILLAN
A Simon & Schuster Macmillan Company
1633 Broadway
New York, NY 10019-6785

MACMILLAN is a registered trademark of Macmillan, Inc.

Library of Congress Cataloging-in-Publication Data available upon request

ISBN 0-02-860386-9

Book design by Vertigo Design

Manufactured in the United States of America
10 9 8 7 6 5 4 3 2 1

Acknowledgments

The editors of *Vegetarian Times* would like to thank: Lillian Kayte, who designed the great-tasting menu for beginning vegetarians in Chapter 3 and who helped in the writing of this book; and Anthony Jaros, who spent many hours pulling together the entire project and without whom this book would not be possible. We'd also like to thank our Special Projects Editor Carol Wiley Lorente, whose expertise in many areas sent us off in the right direction and whose editing helped us focus this book.

—Editors of *Vegetarian Times*

Contents

Introduction

What *is* a vegetarian, anyway?

Sometimes the English language fails us. Take the word "vegetarian." Someone who eats vegetables, right? Yes, but that hardly describes the spectacular variety of vegetables, fruits, and grains that make up a typical vegetarian diet. *Webster's* even describes the adjective "vegetarian," as in "vegetarian diet," as "consisting wholly of vegetables." Wrong.

Even more obtuse is *American Heritage Dictionary's* definition of vegetarianism: "the practice of subsisting on a vegetarian diet." It further describes subsistence as barely sufficient to maintain life.

Vegetarians are used to such slights of the written or spoken word. But someone like you, someone who is thinking of becoming a vegetarian or who is curious about the diet, may not be able to separate fact from myth. For starters, you'll be happy to know that you'll be eating more than vegetables and that you'll be doing more than subsisting. In fact, you'll be heading down a path to good health, and you'll be joining more than 12 million Americans and countless others throughout the world who call themselves vegetarian. In many cases, these millions began just like you; curious about a more healthful, more environmentally friendly way to eat.

What follows in this book is an easy-to-follow guide to a vegetarian diet, and the many reasons why you ought to at least consider a vegetarian lifestyle. Until you read on, you won't know the many benefits that it holds for you and the world around you.

CHAPTER 1

So You Want to Be a Vegetarian

Your interest has been piqued, at least to some degree. Maybe it's because you're curious by nature. Maybe it's because you're tired of what eating hot dogs and french fries is doing to your waistline and your sense of well-being.

Or maybe it's because you want to do something for the planet and the animals that share it with us. The reason really isn't important, but the fact that you've picked up this book is. You're thinking about becoming a vegetarian, and you're wondering what it's all about.

Being a vegetarian means many different things to many different people, and we aren't here to judge anyone's motives. What we *are* here to do is provide information about why a vegetarian diet is one of the best choices you can make for everyone and everything that surrounds you. Over time there have been many myths, strange notions, and downright untruths about a meatless diet held by people who were unfamiliar with a dinner plate that didn't have a piece of chicken or steak dominating it. Turning what may be staunch skepticism into well-grounded knowledge is our goal by way of clearing up the misconceptions that many hold about the "v-word."

This book is not the be-all and end-all of vegetarianism. That would take a thick volume, one that would probably scare you away and make you swear that you never want to see another vegetable in your life. It is instead a guide for anyone starting out on the road to a meatless diet, an introduction, if you will, to the various components of a vegetarian lifestyle. Whether you choose to take baby steps toward giving up meat or plunge headfirst into vegetarianism is up to you. We're fairly sure, however, that once you read on, you'll want to hop in your car and drive to the nearest fresh produce stand or natural food store.

Cast Away Those Stereotypes

IT'S SATURDAY MORNING, and you're wheeling your cart around the grocery store, stocking up for the week. As you bring your items up to the checkout counter, you happen to gaze into the cart of the woman in front of you. You see familiar items: leafy green lettuce; red, ripe tomatoes; fresh green beans; and a beautiful loaf of whole wheat bread. There also are some things with which you aren't too familiar: some curious-looking vegetables and a package with the word "TOFU" in big black letters. What's more, try as you might, you don't notice any ground beef, chicken legs, or thick steaks wrapped in cellophane anywhere in the cart. You stop and wonder for a second. Is this

woman a vegetarian? Could that be? Why does she look so healthy and together? Isn't she supposed to look sickly and pale, dressed in tie-dye and
wearing sandals?

People go vegetarian for a number of reasons:

Health	46 %
Animal welfare	15 %
Influence of family or friends	12 %
Ethical reasons	5 %
Environmental concerns	4 %
Other	9 %

SOURCE: YANKELOVICH PARTNERS STUDY, 1992

The reality is that most vegetarians are just like you, your friends, and
your family. They come in all shapes and sizes, including students, secretaries,
corporate presidents, writers, doctors, lawyers, teachers, mothers, fathers,
sons, and daughters. The last time we counted (1992), there were 12.4 million
people who called themselves vegetarians. Many more are well on their way
toward eliminating meat from their diet, and the number is growing by the
thousands each and every month.

The word "vegetarian" wasn't coined until 1847 by The Vegetarian Society
of the United Kingdom, but the practice stretches way back to ancient Hindu
teachings and to figures like Pythagoras (580–500 B.C.), the renowned Greek
mathematician and philosopher who founded the science of arithmetic and
harmonics and made many discoveries in geometry.

Since ancient times, the vegetarian community has contained many
celebrities and other figures of importance. These include George Bernard
Shaw, Percy Bysshe Shelley, and his wife, Mary, who originally created her
monster in *Frankenstein* as a vegetarian. There have been authors and scientists through the ages, starting with Ovid, Plato, and Plutarch and moving on
to Isaac Newton. Just a few of the hundreds of contemporary vegetarian per-
sonalities include singer Paul McCartney, tennis player Martina Navratilova,
and actress Kim Basinger.

From this wide range of "members," you can see that vegetarians are a group that includes individuals of all sizes, shapes, colors, ages, walks of life, and religious beliefs. This group has no requirements for membership and no profile for an average member. Everyone is always welcome (and tie-dye is optional, but still always well received).

Getting the Jump on Good Health

ONLY TWO DECADES AGO, people were asking why in the world they would want to give up meat. Today, many of these same folks want to know how they can go meatless and, moreover, why no one told them to do it a long time ago. You can see how health-conscious our culture has become just by taking a trip to your local grocery store, where the words "natural," "fat-free," and "meatless" pop out at you. In the past, manufacturers and store owners did little to promote the healthful aspects of their products. Natural food stores used to be scarce, intimidating, and otherwise weird; now they have started to trickle into the mainstream with names like Fresh Fields, Bread & Circus, and Mrs. Gooch's. Healthful living is now a big business, accounting for more than $6 billion worth of today's food market share. While that translates only to about 1.5 percent of the United States' total grocery spending, it is a figure that has risen 120 percent in the last decade, according to *Natural Foods Merchandiser* magazine.

The reason we mention these facts is to demonstrate how easy it has become to find a multitude of foods to supplant meat in your diet. And now that you know how easy it will be to find the foods you need and want, think about the reasons, level of your commitment, and timetable for your switch. Ask yourself these three questions, and don't worry; there are no right or wrong answers.

> Fifty-six percent of U.S. shoppers have reported decreasing their use of beef.
> *Source: HealthFocus, 1993*

Why do I want to become a vegetarian?

How will becoming a vegetarian change my life?

How quickly do I want to make the transition?

If you kick the habit all at once, congratulations—you're a vegetarian. If you do it gradually, eliminating red meat first, then poultry, fish, and shellfish, you'll be more in the mainstream way of doing things. And even if you decide not to give up meat totally but cut back your intake of animal products substantially, you've still done your body—and the environment—some degree of service. No one is going to hover over you and judge the commitment you make. The bottom line is that no one cares about your health quite as much as you do, because no one else has so much at stake.

Let's use some logic. If you start with clean (grown without pesticides), whole (unprocessed) foods that are high in fiber and low in fat, you're enhancing your chances of living a longer, healthier life. These unrefined, clean, whole, fiber-filled, and generally low-fat foods are the grains, fruits, and vegetables that are the basic building blocks of a vegetarian diet, the foods that supply all the nutrition, calories, and energy that we as humans need to survive and thrive.

> Eating processed, prepared foods is expensive—even if they are meatless. Buy grains in bulk and seasonal produce, and make as much as you can yourself. Then if you want to splurge on extra-juicy organic blackberries or time-saving convenience foods, do so with a clear conscience. You're likely saving plenty on medical bills.

Many practicing vegetarians will tell you that their transition was very easy, mostly because they didn't realize how big of a part grains, fruits, and vegetables played in their meat-based diets. There's a pretty good chance you are much the same, halfway or more toward your goal. If you currently eat pasta, cereal, breads, peas, beans, corn, rice, potatoes, and mixed salads, you've got quite a good start. The rest is little more than learning about nutritional, wholesome food and being aware of how what you eat affects the way you feel. Soon it will become automatic. You'll find that eating healthfully is something you won't have to make a special effort to do.

You'll find from talking to other vegetarians that everyone's timetable differs. One of the reasons is that the attachment to meat is not physical but is emotional. Much of how you feel about meat depends on how much you identify with certain foods on special occasions. You know what we mean—the turkey at Thanksgiving, the ham at Easter, or Mom's pot roast on Sunday. Once you can stop associating the presence of meat with every dining occasion, and instead have vegetables, fruits, and grains in its place, you can start your own personal process toward breaking this all-important emotional connection. It may be something you never totally overcome, but at least you can resist the temptation in your moments of doubt.

We suggest a gradual start, then a little self-test after a month or so. After a month of not being weighed down by a load of fat and cholesterol, chances are you'll find you would rather have some savory black bean enchiladas, a robust vegetarian chili, or a snappy stir-fry rather than a hot dog, steak, or hamburger. Chances are you'll find that you really don't miss meat as much as you thought you would. In most new vegetarians, there is a strong sense of pride and accomplishment at setting a goal and then attaining it. Every week that you're able to stay with your vegetarian diet will make you feel better, both physically and emotionally.

There's More to Being a Vegetarian than Just Good Health

TALK TO A DOZEN VEGETARIANS and you'll get any number of different reasons why they made the switch. For some people, it can be to protect the welfare of animals. For others, it might be concern for the disappearing rain forests and depletion of the earth's resources. Still others cite ethical, religious, or spiritual reasons for making the switch from meat to wheat. But for the majority (nearly 50 percent) of vegetarians it starts with what we've focused on so far—a desire to better their overall health and feeling of well-being.

Good health is a terrific reason to be a vegetarian, especially when one medical study after another has sung the praises of a grain- and vegetable-based diet and has recommended that we step up our fiber intake through vegetables, fruits, grains, and beans while taking in less fat through meat and certain dairy products. If you haven't seen the articles supporting a vegetarian diet at the newsstand or the library recently, it's probably just because you haven't been looking. Try *The Journal of the American Medical Association, Time,* or *Newsweek.* Or just about any other title out there.

And while you're reading about all of the great health reasons to become, or stay, a vegetarian, you'll probably stumble across a funny thing about vegetarianism. Just as soon as you think you've found its most compelling advantage, someone else comes up with a little piece of news that makes you feel even better that you made your decision in the first place. Maybe because they are constantly explaining themselves, vegetarians are constantly reading and learning more about the lifestyle they have grown to love. Over time, those vegetarians who gave up meat for health reasons are exposed to information from animal-rights and environmental organizations, and learn, for instance, about the horrible conditions under which most factory farm animals live. (For more information about this topic see Chapter 5, page 143.) Throughout their lives, many vegetarians continue to eat the way they do for reasons that are less personal and more global. Say, for instance, you decide to eat less meat for health reasons. Take a look at how you are helping to reduce some of these very real, very frightening environmental and food facts:

1. Some 64 percent of American agricultural land is used to grow livestock feed.

2. Grain and soybeans that are now fed to U.S. livestock could feed 1.3 billion people.

3. To get one calorie of protein from soybeans, two calories of fossil fuel are expended. To get one calorie of protein from beef, 78 calories of fossil fuel are expended.

4. The water it takes to raise one cow could float a destroyer.

It's easy to see why a vegetarian diet is a friend to the environment: It requires fewer resources. Instead of growing grain to feed the animals you plan to eat, you just eat the grain.

Even if these ecological concerns mean rather little to you at this time, or you're not interested in becoming a full-time vegetarian but simply in cutting back on how much meat you eat, reading this book may positively alter some of your behaviors, thus doing you (and the earth) some good. In fact, if there were more vegetarians, meat production would have no choice but to slow down, and quite possibly some of these social and environmental problems would be alleviated.

As an added incentive, going vegetarian can be cost-efficient, depending on how you go about it. Pesticide-free organic produce generally costs more than regular supermarket produce, but, on the other hand, organic, hormone-free meat is similarly expensive. Doing some quick comparison shopping shows that you can buy quite a few vegetables, rices, and pastas for the same $10 it costs to buy a roast. On your next shopping trip, try it yourself. Use the $10 you would have spent on that roast and spend it on vegetables and grains; then see how full your cart is in comparison.

Safety First

AS A VEGETARIAN, you'll have many different kinds of diet choices. Each one will affect your health in a positive way; one can save your life. When you give up meat, you also avoid the various types of bacteria that often come with it courtesy of speedy modern processing-plant procedures and the insufficient inspection that goes along with them. In the meat industry, speed spells profit, and profit is, of course, what big business in this country is built on. The stories of various food poisonings have dotted newspapers and television broadcasts for several years, each one scarier than the last.

We find ourselves mired in this food scare for reasons that date back to outmoded meat inspection practices established in the 1930s. Further deregulation of the meat-inspection industry by the U.S. Department of Agriculture in the early 1980s only compounded the problem. The immediate goal of the deregulation was to increase the amount of meat that was produced, and it succeeded by a whopping 45 percent. The end result has become all too clear, however, as unsafe meat continues to slip through the system at an alarming rate. Although high heat can kill harmful microbes, at least 9,000 people in the United States get sick every year from contaminated meat and poultry. Of these 9,000, approximately 500 die, and another 6,500 of the survivors will never fully regain their health.

To further fuel this problem, contamination of another sort starts long before the animal reaches the processing plants. Cows, chickens, and pigs are routinely dosed with some eighty kinds of antibiotics. In addition to treating and preventing infections with daily feedings of these antibiotics, farmers routinely use a variety of drugs to make animals grow bigger and faster per pound of feed used. This flood of antibiotics has led to a slew of recent reports on the effects this treated meat has on humans, and the possibility that some bacterial diseases have become resistant to what has been known to many as a common cure-all. When you eat animal flesh, it then becomes part of you, antibiotics, pesticides, and all. It can be that simple, and that scary.

In addition to caring about how we treat our own bodies, it is difficult to turn a blind eye to the treatment animals receive on present-day American factory farms. When we were children in school, we were taught about how cows and chickens on farms roamed freely and spent long, happy lives until they were one day used (out of extreme necessity) for human consumption. The harsh truth is that the majority of factory farms treat their animals brutally all the days of their lives until they are even more brutally killed. For the millions of cows, chickens, pigs, calves, sheep, and lambs that are kept in grossly overcrowded and filthy pens, the sun never shines; they live in a world of darkness, fear, and pain. The truthful pictures and depictions of real farm life may be enough in and of themselves to turn you off to meat forever.

Do I Have to Eat Salad Every Day?

TWO WORDS: NO WAY. You have a nearly endless array of full-flavored grains from all over the globe, some of them dating from antiquity like millet and quinoa (KEEN-wa); pastas plain and fancy; beans of every shape, size, and color; peas; filling winter vegetables and light crunchy summertime ones; and fruits and berries in all the colors of the rainbow. And with a little help from our recipe chapter, you'll find it's easy to bring them all together in marvelous innovative ways now that vegetarian cooking has caught the attention of mainstream chefs and other food professionals.

There's not a chance of becoming bored with the variety of fresh fruits and vegetables that are available year round. Use them in salads, stir-fries, soups, stews, side dishes, main dishes, casseroles, desserts, spreads, and dips. Mother Nature has done a marvelous job of matching your tastes and energy level to each and every season, so choose your food in season for maximum taste and nutritive value. Like many people, you'll probably tend toward cool, crisp cucumbers and melons in the summer, and the heartier textures of winter squashes and root vegetables in fall and winter. Don't forget to include lots of leafy green vegetables like kale, collards, mixed lettuces, and mustard, turnip, and beet greens, plus cancer-fighting cruciferous vegetables like broccoli, brussels sprouts, cabbage, and cauliflower all year long.

You'll learn how to use plants instead of meats to create satisfying meals. And contrary to popular belief, vegetables and fruits do not play the only role in a vegetarian diet. Think of them more as side dishes used to dress up and complement the grains and starches that are the true building blocks of most meatless entrées.

What's to Come

WE'VE DESIGNED THIS BOOK as sort of a road map on your journey toward becoming a vegetarian, eating less meat, or whatever else you want the journey to be. In the next chapter, "Vegetarianism 101," we formally introduce you to the basics of a vegetarian diet, as well as to some of the new and different foods that you'll encounter. We'll try to dispel some of the popular myths and misconceptions about vegetarianism, such as the outdated notions that a meatless diet does not provide adequate protein, iron, or calcium. Other topics covered include the pros and cons of drinking milk, why reading labels is important and how to make the new labeling system work best for you, and whether or not supplements need to be a mainstay in your medicine chest.

By the time you get the hang of this easy-to-understand nutrition information, we'll head you into Chapter 3, "Ready, Set, Eat!," and get you started with meal planning, shopping, cooking, and (finally!) eating. To give you a hand with those first few meals, and to demonstrate just a bit of the variety a vegetarian diet brings, we've prepared two weeks of menus, complete with shopping lists, on pages 64–112. Cooking up just a few of these delicious meatless entrées is the best way to convince even the biggest disbeliever that vegetarian food isn't boring and bland. In addition to the recipes, Chapter 3 will review some basic techniques of cooking vegetables in order for you to prepare the best-tasting, most nutritious vegetables that you possibly can. We'll include a guide to some quick vegetarian convenience foods for those who are always on the go, but still want to eat a healthful diet, and provide some tips to help you make more efficient use of the time you spend in the kitchen.

In Chapter 4, "It's Time for Some *Real* Health-Care Reform," we'll synthesize the issues of food, nutrition, and health, and examine why a low-fat, vegetarian diet is helpful not only in the recovery from some diseases and conditions but also in acting to prevent them. From heart disease to cancer to diabetes, Americans could save lives and money by simply making some basic changes in their diet. We'll also discuss how exercise is vital to a healthy individual and give you some suggestions on how to start your own exercise program as soon as possible.

In Chapter 5, "Compassionate, Clean, and Green," we look at more of the positive aspects of a vegetarian diet—the preservation of the environment and the alleviation of terrible animal suffering. We'll show you how to buy smarter to avoid excess trash with a view toward recycling, how to live in an Earth-friendly way, how to buy cruelty-free personal and household products, and where to get literature to participate in various green and animal-welfare groups. We'll also introduce some other subjects that are important to vegetarians, such as tree planting, water conservation, and pesticide-free farming.

Finally, in Chapter 6, "Special Circumstances, Special Solutions," we'll research whether or not a vegetarian diet is still appropriate for special groups such as pregnant mothers, young children, teenagers, the elderly, and, yes, even your pets! We'll also discuss how to maintain a meat-free diet when you're away from home, whether it be for business or pleasure, and how to handle some of the social situations that may be uncomfortable for new vegetarians.

It's All Up to You

WE'RE HERE TO PROVIDE YOU with the basic information, the tools you will need to decide whether a meatless diet is right for you. But this is only the beginning. You need to be smart, know your own body, your own reasons, and your own goals. Know what you're buying before you buy it. Read the labels, set your limits, and buy whole unprocessed, unrefined foods whenever possible. And remember, if you set out believing that just giving up meat without thinking about what you're putting into your mouth will lead to a balanced diet, forget it. You need to make a conscious effort to improve your eating habits, your exercise habits, and, in turn, your quality of life. The fact that this book devotes long sections to issues such as health and environmental consciousness just goes to show that there is much more to vegetarianism than food. Making a commitment to vegetarianism means making a commitment to a life that is by its very nature more healthful and compassionate.

Finally, since we hope this book will be the beginning of a long-term relationship between you and the rewarding world of meatless cooking, we're going to give you a list of our favorite books on each topic we discuss, so you can head to the library in the hopes of expanding on the knowledge we are providing here. These are the best no-nonsense books for beginners, the kind we use every day and the kind that will give you the best introductory and intermediate information to the vegetarian lifestyle.

As you read on, you'll begin to see the simplicity, fun, and many rewards of being a vegetarian. You'll discover that, contrary to the belief that you'll be giving up something, you'll be gaining more than you ever dreamed possible.

CHAPTER 2

Vegetarianism 101

Y OU'RE AT A PARTY, AND THE HOSTESS IS WANDERING ABOUT WITH A

DISH OF BARBECUED COCKTAIL WEENIES. SHE APPROACHES YOU AND HOLDS

THE DISH UNDER YOUR NOSE. YOU DECLINE POLITELY, BUT SHE INSISTS—

EVERYONE ALWAYS LOVES THEM. YOU BEGIN TO SWEAT AND SHIFT NERVOUSLY IN

YOUR SHOES. QUIETLY YOU SAY THAT YOU'RE REALLY NOT INTERESTED—

YOU'RE A VEGETARIAN.

"Vegetarian!" she cries. "When did *you* become a vegetarian?" A hush falls over the room as everyone stares at you as if you'd grown a second head. A psychologist moves closer in the hopes of capturing you for what he calls "just a little mental testing." Someone else tries to lighten the situation by yelling out, "What are you, some kind of tree-hugging liberal?" Another concerned observer speaks up: "You *can't* be getting enough protein. Or iron. Or calcium. Aren't you afraid you'll get sick?"

Though staying at the party may seem as appetizing as those weenies, stick to your beliefs and resist the temptation to head for the nearest door. Spend some time talking to the partygoers and trying to dispel some popular misconceptions about vegetarians. You'll find out soon enough that the comments are rooted in a lack of information, not malice.

To be able to satisfy the questions and doubts that you and others may have, it helps to get some solid information about a vegetarian diet. We're sure you want to know all about what types of foods you'll be eating and how those foods provide you with all the nutrition you need. You'll find the answers to these and many other questions about vegetarianism in this chapter. Remember, being educated about your body and what you put into it (or choose not to put into it) is knowledge that is valuable for a lifetime of health and happiness.

These Are the People Who Are Vegetarians

THE FIRST THING YOU should know about being a vegetarian is that you have more than one choice of who you want to be. There are a few different types of vegetarians, which are explained below. Part-time vegetarians, people who say, "I'm a vegetarian—I'm only eating red meat once a month," really don't fit into any of these groups. These people are considered to be in transition, interested in eating more healthfully and potentially on their way toward eliminating animal products altogether.

Here is a rundown of the three groups:

Ovo-Lacto Vegetarians. Possibly the most popular choice among new vegetarians. They do not eat any animal flesh but do use dairy products and eggs.

Lacto Vegetarians. Do not eat any animal flesh or eggs but do use dairy products.

Vegans (VEE-guns or VEJ-ens). The most complete of all vegetarians, vegans do not eat animal products of any type, including animal flesh (red meat, chicken, pork, fish, or shellfish), dairy products, eggs, or honey.

Back to Grade School

IF YOU'RE LIKE MOST PEOPLE, you were taught from an early age to follow the "traditional" four basic food groups or the newer food pyramid if you wanted a complete diet. It's no secret that meat, poultry, and other animal products have been staples in both of these nutrition schematics for as long as they've been around. But now that you're giving up meat, you may be worried that your pyramid will be a trapezoid or that your four food groups are one short, breaking the mold of what you have known as the "right" way to eat for so long. Take heart—this switch in thinking makes many nervous, and we're well prepared to calm your fears. Once you get the right information, you'll find that for nearly every question or challenge, vegetarians have a well-grounded answer to more than justify eating and living the way they do, both to themselves and others.

For example, as an alternative to the familiar government food pyramid, the nutrition council of the Seventh-Day Adventist Church, which has advocated a vegetarian diet for more than 100 years, has developed its own pyramid. Following the recommended diet in both pyramids will provide components of nutrition that health practitioners and government officials recommend, but meat is conspicuously absent from the Seventh-Day version. Meat and its nutritional value can be effectively replaced in your diet, which is a pretty good tradeoff—better nutrition without the harmful side effects. Here are the two pyramids for comparison:

U.S. Government Food Pyramid

Meats, Poultry, Fish, Dried Beans and Peas, Eggs, and Nuts

Dairy Products

Vegetables and Fruits

Breads, Cereals, Rice, and Pasta

Seventh-Day Adventist Food Pyramid

Fats, Oils, and Sweets

Milk, Yogurt, Cheese, Beans, Nuts, Seeds, and Meat Alternatives

Vegetables and Fruits

Whole Grains, Breads, Cereals, Rice, and Pasta

No amount of repetition can underscore the importance of a diet that is built upon whole grains and vegetables. But while the government pyramid also recommends eating meats, poultry, and fish, vegetarians know that the fat and cholesterol contained in these foods is better avoided.

Even though the government pyramid has been somewhat updated from the one you may have known as a child, it still contains many of the inadequacies and oddities for which it has been long criticized, such as the placement of beans near the top of the pyramid, meaning they should be eaten only about as much as meat products (two to three servings per day). Beans, however, are one of nature's most perfect foods, low in fat and cholesterol and high in protein and fiber. They should be eaten fairly liberally, but since the government views them as a source of protein (which meat also provides), they are lumped into a group that is better off not eaten at all. One final note about the government pyramid is that although highly processed or refined foods often qualify as a serving, refined and processed cookies and crackers are really devoid of truly substantial nutritive value. Some government analyses, however, plop them square into the breads and grains category. Vegetarian nutrition plans focus on natural, not refined, foods that are in their purest state and thus are our best sources of vitamins and minerals.

Developed separately but complementing the vegetarian pyramid are four new food groups that have been created by Neal Barnard, a Washington, D.C., doctor who advocates nutrition reform through a vegetarian diet. Tossing aside the old meat, dairy, grains, and greens setup, Barnard proposes these as the groups from which we should be getting breakfast, lunch, and dinner:

Vegetables (three or more servings per day)

Fruits (three or more servings per day)

Whole grains (five or more servings per day)

Legumes (two or more servings per day)

We're fairly certain that you have a pretty good grasp on what your basic lettuce, tomatoes, and cucumbers are, but there is much more to the fruits and vegetable group than that. Likewise, there is more to the grains group than Wonder Bread and more to the legumes group than canned green beans. Our recipes in the next chapter will have you experimenting with some new foods in ways with which you may be unfamiliar. Later in this chapter, we'll take a look at some of these foods, but first we need to take a look at how a vegetarian diet can provide you with the nutrition you need.

Debunking the Myths

GO BACK A MOMENT to our cocktail party earlier in the chapter, where one of the well-meaning partygoers questioned whether a vegetarian diet could be nutritionally sound. Are you, by forsaking meat, forsaking the necessary vitamins, minerals, and other nutrients you need to be healthy? These questions, and the worries that accompany them, are common for many new vegetarians. Even vegetarians of many, many years still may have a nagging doubt from time to time when they're feeling a little under the weather, and their meat-eating coworkers are feeling fit as a fiddle and gently ribbing them about their lifestyle.

Without a doubt, the first question to be asked and the last answer to be accepted is how vegetarians can possibly get the protein they need. There has

been no nutrient over the past fifty years that has dominated American tables in the way that protein has. From early childhood, many of us remember adults being fixated on it, telling us we needed more if we wanted to be strong and healthy. But what Mom and Dad should have known is that protein deficiency in this country is so rare that many nutritionists and doctors wouldn't even know the symptoms if they were faced with them.

The first thing to understand about protein is what it doesn't do. It doesn't make you feel energetic. That's the role of carbohydrates. And it doesn't build muscle. Good old exercise is responsible for that. Protein *is* a very important nutrient. It helps you think and see, repairs bone and muscle tissue, regulates hormones and enzymes, helps fight infections, and affects your genes and chromosomes, among other functions. But if you're feeling a bit lethargic, too little protein isn't the reason. If you think you may want to tone up a little bit, eating more protein won't help you. You'd be better off to take a walk, eat some pasta, or lift some weights.

The next thing to know is that all recent research indicates that if you're eating enough calories in a day, which most of us are, you're getting enough protein. This is because *every food*, with the exception of fruit, fat, and sugar, has protein in it. And finally, the last thing to know about protein is that as an average American, you're probably getting far more than the U.S. government's Recommended Dietary Allowance (RDA) per day. The RDA for protein for an American man aged thirty to fifty-nine is sixty-three grams, yet the average intake for a man in this category is ninety-three grams per day. The RDA for a woman aged thirty to fifty-nine is fifty grams, but the average woman in this category is taking in sixty-five grams per day. You may wonder what the problem is, as we're taught the more protein the better, but there is something our schooling left out. Research shows that an excess of protein is bad (we repeat, *bad*) for the human body. The least serious effect of excessive protein consumption is that your body will convert it to waste. But a protein "overload" can actually reduce the body's ability to absorb calcium, which may result in osteoporosis or even, in some cases, kidney disease.

Another supposed phenomenon that links vegetarians to problems with protein is a term that is commonly known as protein complementing. The term was brought into the public eye by Frances Moore Lappé in her 1971 book *Diet for a Small Planet*. In it, Lappé described how protein is constructed of tiny strands of amino acids, twenty of which have been identified as important to the human body. Our bodies manufacture eleven out of these twenty amino acids with no assistance; the remaining nine must be taken in through the consumption of food. Lappé correctly pointed out that all plant-based foods are lacking in one of the nine remaining amino acids (different foods lack different amino acids, depending on their chemical makeup). She concluded that vegetarians, if they wanted to make sure they took in the rest of the nine essential amino acids, would have to "complement" a low-protein food with a food that was high in the amino acid that vegetable lacked. For example, rice is low in the amino acid lysine, while beans are low in methionine. Eating both in combination would theoretically make up for one or the other's deficiency. This set vegetarians out on a quest to be always mindful of what they were eating, so as not to cheat their bodies. But since no one eats only one food per day, by eating a variety of foods and getting enough calories, people are automatically eating complete protein.

Research done on protein in the ten years following Lappé's work confirmed this fact and helped prove that complementing was unnecessary. Lappé, in her revised version of *Diet* in 1981, reversed her stand on protein complementing, but still, the protein question continues to haunt vegetarians. To make matters worse, some books, food magazines, and so-called experts continue to perpetuate the myth despite Lappé's valiant efforts to bring people up to date.

The reality is that one cup of legumes such as beans or peas delivers between thirteen and sixteen grams of protein, with some beans packing a

SOME COMMON SOURCES OF PROTEIN

Food	Serving Size	Grams (g)
Almonds	2 ounces (24 nuts)	6.5
Avocado	1 medium	5.6
Beans, kidney	½ cup cooked	7.2
Bread, white	1 slice	2.4
Broccoli	½ cup cooked	2.4
Bulgur	1 cup cooked	8.4
Cheese, cheddar	1 ¼ ounces	15.5
Cheese, cottage	½ cup	15
Cornmeal	1 cup	11.2
Eggs	2 medium	11.4
Lentils	½ cup cooked	7.8
Milk, skim	8 ounces	8.8
Oatmeal	1 cup cooked in water	4.8
Peanut butter	2 tablespoons	8
Potato	7 ounces baked	4
Rice, brown	1 cup cooked	4.9
Soybeans	½ cup cooked	9.9
Tofu	4 ounces	10
Wheat, shredded	2 biscuits	5
Yogurt	8 ounces	8.3

walloping twenty nine grams per cup. So, based on the government RDAs, getting enough protein is a piece of cake. What should be more important to you is the fact that from the body's point of view, there's no difference in the amount of protein found in one-half cup of soybeans and that found in five ounces of steak. But while the protein content is exactly the same, the steak would tally up to four or five times as many calories and bring with it some sixteen grams of artery-clogging fat. If you can get the same protein from another source that isn't harmful to your system, why not do it?

The Rumor Mill, Continued

As a new vegetarian, you'll probably find yourself fielding more questions about your diet than just protein intake. Meat eaters also are baffled to find that vegetarians are perfectly capable of getting all the nutrients they need, even iron and calcium, which most of us picture as coming only from animal sources such as meat or milk. Let's take a look at both iron and calcium to get to the bottom of all these claims.

Iron is another of our most essential nutrients. Its primary function is to transport oxygen in the blood. Most of the iron in our system is stored as a part of hemoglobin, the red blood cell protein that transports oxygen to tissues. While our bodies are quite efficient at recycling iron, over time we lose some and need to replace it. To remain in a state of iron balance, we must absorb enough iron from food to replace the iron we lose. This is particularly true of women who are menstruating, because they lose blood on a monthly basis; they are therefore more likely to be iron-deficient. Iron deficiency happens to be the most prevalent nutritional problem in the world, which is strange considering that iron is abundant both in the earth and in our food supply. In First World societies such as the United States, scientists estimate that 5 percent to 10 percent of women of childbearing age and teenagers are iron-deficient.

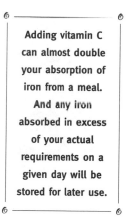

Adding vitamin C can almost double your absorption of iron from a meal. And any iron absorbed in excess of your actual requirements on a given day will be stored for later use.

Eating meat has long been viewed as the best way to obtain dietary iron, but that view may now be changing. In the past, however, articles published in scientific journals and the lay press have erroneously reported a link between a vegetarian diet and iron deficiency, something that may be due to improper interpretation of epidemiological study data. Iron deficiency is most common in Third World nations, where diets are predominantly plant- or cereal-based due to lower economic conditions and the subsequent absence of meat. This

THE CURRENT RDAS for iron are: Infants up to 6 months, 6 milligrams; children 6 months to 10 years, 10 milligrams; women from 11 to 50 years, 15 milligrams; women over 50 years, 10 milligrams; pregnant women, 30 milligrams; men up to 18 years, 12 milligrams; men over 18 years, 10 milligrams.

Some common sources of iron:

Food	Serving Size	Milligrams (mg)
Fruits		
Figs	10	4.2
Mulberries	1 cup	2.6
Prunes	10	2.4
Raisins, seedless	1/2 cup	1.7
Apricots, dried halves	10	1.7
Vegetables		
Belgian endive	1 head (6 inches)	7
Spinach, cooked	1 cup	4
Swiss chard	1 cup	3.2
Dandelion greens or kale, cooked	1 cup	2
Winter squash, baked	1 cup	1.4
Beets, cooked	1 cup	1.3
Legumes		
Black-eyed peas, cooked	1/2 cup	3.8
Lentils, cooked	1/2 cup	3.4
Kidney beans, cooked	1/2 cup	3.3
Lima beans, cooked	1/2 cup	2.9
Grains		
Quinoa, cooked	1 cup	5.3

Grains (*continued*)

Millet, cooked	1 cup	2.2
Cracked wheat, cooked	1 cup	2

Other

Blackstrap molasses	2 tablespoons	4.6
Sesame seeds, unhulled	2 tablespoons	2
Nutritional yeast	1 tablespoon	1.4

Some common sources of calcium:

Food	Serving Size	Milligrams (mg)
Almonds, dry roasted	1 ounce	80
Beans, red	1 cup	81
Beans, white	1 cup	226
Blackstrap molasses	2 tablespoons	274
Broccoli, cooked	1 cup	132
Brussels sprouts	1 cup	128
Collard greens, cooked	1 cup	356
Kale, cooked	1 cup	204
Milk	1 cup	300
Okra, cooked	1 cup	147
Orange juice (calcium fortified)	8 ounces	320
Sesame seeds, unhulled	2 tablespoons	218
Spinach, cooked	1 cup	244
Tofu (coagulated with calcium sulfate)	½ cup	258
Turnip greens, cooked	1 cup	252
Winter squash, baked	1 cup	57

Sources: *New Laurel's Kitchen* (Ten Speed Press, 1986) and *Dietary Calcium: Adequacy of a Vegetarian Diet* by Connie Weaver and Karen Plawecki.

coincidence seemed to be enough for some researchers, who immediately jumped to the conclusion that a plant-based diet leads to iron deficiency.

A little more digging ould have revealed that the problem with most Third World diets is not the absence of meat but the absence of sources of ascorbic acid, or vitamin C. Ascorbic acid helps us absorb iron, whether we eat meat or not. The combination of a healthy intake of iron along with the vitamin C you need is the key. If you are a vegetarian and eat poorly, you run a higher risk of being iron deficient, just as you do with a meat-based diet that is low in vitamin C.

There is one hitch. Dietary iron comes in two forms, heme and nonheme. About half the iron in red meat is heme iron; lesser amounts of it are in both poultry and fish. The body readily absorbs heme iron, but plant foods contain only nonheme iron, which the body has a more difficult time absorbing. The average person will absorb 2 percent to 20 percent of iron in plant foods, but 15 percent to 35 percent of iron from meat. This doesn't mean you should drop this book and head for a hamburger. It's still easy for your body to get the iron you need; you just have to give it a little help. Eat plant foods that have iron in them, and help your body absorb the nonheme iron in those foods by making sure you're taking in some vitamin C. In other words, have a glass of orange juice with breakfast and sprinkle some raisins on your cereal. Not too difficult, right? Once your body has absorbed the iron, it can't tell whether it came from either plant- or animal-based foods. And as with protein, you have spared your heart and arteries the cholesterol and saturated fat that come with animal-based products.

VITAMIN C SOURCES

Food	Serving Size	Vitamin C (mg)
Orange juice, fresh	1 cup	124
Broccoli, boiled	1 cup	116
Brussels sprouts, cooked	1 cup	97
Red bell peppers, raw	1/2 cup	95
Cantaloupe	1 cup cubes	68

SOURCE: PREVENTION'S FOOD AND NUTRITION (RODALE PRESS, 1993)

You Don't Have to Wear a Flower in Your Hair

OF COURSE THERE are other myths, none of them as serious as whether you're getting the proper nutrition, but fun to play along with all the same. No, all vegetarians are not whacked-out health nuts who live on vitamins, tofu, and seaweed. Like anyone else, some vegetarians believe in taking vitamin supplements; others can't remember the last time they had one. And although it's true that most vegetarians gravitate toward vegetarian food for its health benefits, there are vegetarians who think Spaghetti-Os with a chaser of root beer is a good meal. To each his own.

Vegetarians are not a homogeneous cult, either. In fact, there are so many kinds of vegetarians we could never count. And while some vegetarians (like anyone) want to preach about the style of life they're living, for the most part you'll never find a friendlier group that is more eager to share knowledge. Being a vegetarian is kind of like being in a club that is inclusive and caring about everyone and everything, from your health to the state of the earth to the conditions under which farm animals live. There are no requirements—just a willingness to listen, consider, and possibly change.

Vegetarian foods that are high in iron include beans, dried fruits (such as raisins), green leafy vegetables (such as spinach and kale), grains (such as quinoa and rye flour), and herbs (such as sage and alfalfa). Truthfully, iron is found in so many plant foods that even if you're not eating the most iron-rich foods, as long as you're taking in enough calories in a day, you're probably getting enough iron. If you're a woman with particularly iron-poor blood, however, you may want to take a supplement that is fortified with iron.

The mysteries of calcium are a bit more complicated to solve. Another popular myth about vegetarians, especially vegans, who do not drink milk, is that they cannot possibly get the calcium they need to keep their bones strong and their bodies healthy. Calcium's main roles are threefold: to promote the normal development of teeth and bones, to maintain bone mass during adulthood, and to minimize the loss of bone mass as we age. Throughout our lifetime, the amount of calcium we need changes, with the highest amount being required during periods of rapid growth, in women when they are pregnant and lactating, and later in our adult lives.

There is little question that we can get calcium from plant-based sources. Broccoli, kale, turnip greens, calcium-fortified tofu, and spinach all have appreciable amounts of calcium inside of them. Grains in the form of bread and cereals, while relatively low in calcium, are still good sources of the mineral because of their high frequency of intake. However, there is currently some debate about just how effectively the body absorbs plant-based calcium as opposed to the high level of calcium absorption when it is derived from animal products. But this all may be counteracted, as we discussed in the section on protein, by the fact that those on a meat-based, high-protein diet absorb less calcium because of their high protein intake, which has been shown to inhibit calcium absorption. Got it straight? Overall, making an effort to drink calcium-fortified juices or soymilks, eating green leafy vegetables that are high in calcium, and keeping your protein at its proper level are the best ways to handle this dilemma until more conclusive proof can be gained.

Dairy—Is It Getting Scary?

ON THE FIRST DAY that moms walked the earth, the first thing out of their mouths probably was: "Finish your milk." That's because since the dawn of Mom, there has always been an expert that will vouch for the nutritional superiority of milk, what with its high levels of protein, vitamin D, and, most important, calcium. And who can fault moms for listening to scientists, especially when for once they seemed to universally agree on something? But they don't agree any longer. A group of dissenters is getting bigger and bigger as some new studies are being done on the old creamy wonder drink.

Milk first came under fire during the 1980s as scientific studies were conducted that found traces of the antibiotic drugs given to dairy cows to keep them healthy and productive. Though the residues were fairly minimal, some experts cautioned that traces of antibiotics such as penicillin could cause reactions in those allergic to the drug. Then a report released in 1992 by the General Accounting Office, the investigative arm of Congress, reported that the

U.S. Food and Drug Administration's (FDA) National Drug Milk Monitoring Program tests for only twelve of the sixty-four drugs that are commonly administered to dairy cows. This left many wondering if we had any way to know just what we are ingesting when we drink a glass of milk.

The milk debate was stoked again in late 1994 as the FDA approved for use in dairy cows a new synthetic growth hormone known as bovine somatotropin, more familiar to many of us as bovine growth hormone, or BGH. Approval of the man-made BGH had been delayed because of evidence that the hormone increased the occurrence of mastitis, an udder infection that is treated with even more antibiotics. There is some evidence that drinking milk that contains low levels of antibiotics may cause the body to develop a resistance to them, diminishing the effectiveness of prescription antibiotics on disease. Many researchers say reduced effectiveness of antibiotics in recent years, partially caused by the public's consistent ingestion of low levels of the drugs, is causing a rebirth of diseases such as tuberculosis, previously thought to be eradicated with the dawn of modern vaccinations.

What does this mean to me, you ask? Maybe nothing, or maybe something, depending on how much these studies scare you, and whether you want to keep dairy products as a part of your vegetarianism. We certainly don't need the saturated fat and cholesterol that most milk contains. A 1-cup serving of 1 percent milk has 100 calories, 10 grams of cholesterol, and 10 percent of your recommended daily saturated fat intake. And now there are even more studies that question whether the vitamins and minerals we have been assured milk contains are actually present at the right levels. Take vitamin D for instance: Recent samples from different milks show that its level can vary dramatically from glass to glass. In a 1993 *New England Journal of Medicine* study, ninety-four milk samples from ten states yielded a range of vitamin D content from undetectable to one sample that had 383 percent more vitamin D than listed on its label. One further note about vitamin D is that it is readily available in many other sources, including merely being exposed to sunlight, according to Michael Murray, N.D., and Joseph Pizzorno, N.D., authors of *The Encyclopedia of Natural Medicine.*

The biggest selling point for milk has always been its calcium, used by children in their bone development, and by adults to prevent bone deterioration, or osteoporosis. Here is where the area regarding milk becomes particularly gray. Some researchers have conducted studies indicating that the body absorbs calcium better from other sources, including broccoli, kale, and bok choy, but others have disagreed, saying that to get the same amount of calcium that you would in a glass of milk, you would have to eat quite a bit of broccoli. Nothing truly conclusive has been gained from any of these studies. Maybe in the coming years that will change. Until that happens, drinking milk remains a careful weighing of the potential pros and cons for both yourself and your family.

Milk Alternatives

ONE OF THE MOST common pitfalls for new vegetarians is that they have a tendency to rely too much on dairy products, particularly milk. This stems from a worry that they need these foods for their all-important calcium and to replace the protein they used to get from meat. But as we know, calcium and protein can easily be obtained from plant foods, so drinking milk becomes more of a personal choice than a nutritional necessity.

So that your cereal won't go dry or your cookies won't be left all alone, there are milk alternatives made from soy, nuts, and rice. All can be bought at your local natural foods store; and if you're industrious, some even can be made at home.

SOYMILK. Soymilk is made by blending soaked whole soybeans with water, and straining out the pulp. The mixture is then cooked, cooled, and flavored. Soymilk that is made with more soybeans per volume of water can be whipped just like cream and can be made into nondairy yogurt and ice cream.

Lightly sweetened vanilla soymilk is great as a beverage and on cereal. Combine it with carob, chocolate, or fresh fruit for thick, rich-tasting shakes and smoothies. Another distinct advantage of soymilks is that they are generally packaged aseptically, which means long shelflife without refrigeration.

One caveat, however: Nondairy doesn't necessarily mean low-fat. Soybeans contain fat, and manufacturers add a little oil in varying amounts for flavor and texture.

NUTMILK. Most any kind of nut can be made into yet another delicious alternative to dairy milk. Nutmilk can be plain or flavored, and should be used chilled as a beverage, or poured over hot and cold cereals. It can also be substituted measure for measure in baking as a replacement for dairy milk. Add it to soups and sauces toward the very end of the cooking time to prevent them from breaking or separating, or whirl it through a blender with fruit and freeze into pops.

> If nutmilk isn't available at your local health food store, make your own by blending a half cup of blanched nuts with two cups of water until very smooth. Add a little sweetener, then pour through a fine mesh strainer. Add one more cup water if desired and chill.

Nutmilk contains no cholesterol, but does have varying amounts of fat. It makes up for the extra fat content by containing powerful nutrients like calcium, phosphorus, protein, folic acid, and more.

RICE MILK, RICE AND SOY BLEND. Rice milk is made from organically grown, partially milled brown rice and, like some soymilks, can contain a small amount of oil. It's a lighter-tasting alternative to soymilk and rich in complex carbohydrates, low in sodium, and cholesterol-free. Soy and rice blend is just what its name implies—a blend of the two non-dairy milks. It can be used in the same way dairy milk is used, both as a beverage and in baking.

The Fat Factor

IT HAD TO COME up sometime. The word that haunts all of us as we pick up that third donut, have one more slice of pizza or one more cookie. Dare we say it—FAT! We know you love fat, and like an old security blanket, you're reluctant to ease your grip. Go ahead, ask your questions now.

Will I, on a vegetarian diet, be eating less fat? Yes.

Is this a good thing? Yes.

Do you need some fat to function? Yes.

Will you miss the fat once you start cooking without it? Probably for a while.

Will a low-fat diet make eating unenjoyable? No.

If you're counting calories, keep in mind that all fats (butter, margarine, oils) have nine calories per gram. Both proteins (meat) and carbohydrates (fruits, vegetables, and grains) have four calories per gram.

Here is how many people who have reduced their fat intake look at the change: Yes, the round "mouth feel" of fat is diminished, but it is replaced by the clear, crisp flavor of what you are eating. No heavy coverups—just fresh, pure flavor. After their palate has had time to adjust, many vegetarians say that fat-laden foods seem not to taste so great; they are heavy and rich without the satisfaction that used to accompany them. It turns out that fat is just a habit like any other, and habits can be broken.

This is in no way an order to cut out all fat. Not only would that take a lot of joy out of eating, but fat is an essential nutrient—not just an optional treat. The "fat-soluble" vitamins—A, D, E, and K—are found in fat. It is possible to get these vitamins from other sources, like supplements, but fat also provides the environment they need to be absorbed, something a supplement cannot do. In addition, fat is important for cell growth and multiplication.

Experts disagree on how much fat you need. Some advise getting no more than 10 percent of your calories from fat, especially if you have (or are in a high-risk group for) heart disease. Many others say 15 percent to 20 percent is a reasonable goal. The official government number is 30 percent of calories from fat, but the average American outdoes them all, getting about 37 percent of his or her calories from fat. That amount is not even close to a diet that promotes a healthy heart in the future. A number closer to 15 percent to 20 percent of calories from fat is a much better goal.

There are two kinds of fats: saturated and unsaturated. If you want to be sure you're eating in a heart-healthy way, try to keep away from saturated fats. "Sat fats," almost exclusively found in animal products, are the ones that end up doing nasty things like clinging to your arteries, causing blockages, and necessitating bypass surgeries. Unsaturated and monounsaturated fats, found in high levels in food like nuts and seeds, are the more desirable kinds of fats to promote the functions described above without causing such a trauma for the system, provided they are eaten in reasonable amounts.

Fat Substitutes

If you think that cutting fat from your diet means that your food will taste bad, think again. With a few simple suggestions, you can reduce the amount of eggs, butter, margarine, and oil you use when cooking and baking.

Fat's primary role in baking is to counteract the effects of gluten, the protein in wheat. Gluten toughens pastry, so we use fat to lift and lighten the gluten and create a tenderness in the baked goods. Knowing this, there are two obvious plans of action: Use a flour with less gluten or change the way you provide that lightness. To reduce the gluten, use whole wheat pastry flours, unbleached white flour, or the newly available white-wheat flours. Most of the time, these flours can be substituted for regular whole wheat flour measure for measure.

> If you can't find prune purée in the grocery store, make your own. Place two cups of pitted prunes in a food processor or blender with four teaspoons of vanilla and three-quarters of a cup of water. Blend to a fine purée. Makes two-and-a-half cups.

Fat also stabilizes a batter's air bubbles, holding them in place as they bake and creating a network of gluten and other ingredients. Anything with a thick, viscous texture (puréed prunes, applesauce, mashed bananas, or tofu) can substitute for egg yolks, nuts, oil, or butter. The most important thing to remember when making these substitutions is to preserve the original balance of wet and dry ingredients. If you remove one-half cup of oil, replace it with the same amount of the chosen substitute. Fat's final role in baking is to carry flavor; if you're substituting, taste the batter to get the flavor you want. You may find that you need more flavorings, spices, or sweeteners as you lower the fat.

When it comes to frying or sautéing, dry sherry, white wine, and red wine are all acceptable substitutes for oil or butter. You can also get nice flavor from apple juice, vegetable broth, or tomato juice. To substitute a liquid for fat in a sauté, use two to four tablespoons of liquid for every tablespoon of oil omitted. Also, remember to simmer the liquid before adding the ingredients. The liquid must be hot enough to coat all the food and seal in the flavors.

We'd Like to Introduce You To . . .

THERE IS A LOT of uncertainty for new vegetarians. They worry about how much they're going to miss their favorite foods from childhood. They worry about whether they're going to be getting the nutrition they need. And they worry, or perhaps are a little frightened, about using new foods to replace meat in dishes they used to cook. Trying new and perhaps strange-looking vegetables may be difficult enough in itself, but opening up that first package of tofu may be downright baffling when you have no idea what tofu is. But tofu and a host of other soyfoods are great meat substitutes for vegetarians in transition, and learning about them and how to use them may make the switch from meat eater to vegetarian that much easier. What's more, researchers are indicating that soyfoods may have cholesterol-reducing properties, which in turn could lessen our risk of high blood pressure and heart disease. Here is a handy guide to some of these foods that you may want to experiment with sooner or later.

Tofu

When you're wandering around the produce aisle and gaze into that small, foreign-food refrigerated section with a host of roots and fruits you've never seen, tofu is that white, jiggling block packed in water that is staring right back at you. It is also known as soybean curd, created when soymilk is separated into curds and whey. These curds are pressed into blocks and then packed into those friendly packages.

Tofu is the most notable and versatile of the soyfoods; a five-ounce serving has only eighty-six calories and yet delivers a whopping ten grams of protein. And like all plant foods, it has no cholesterol. Regular tofu derives 40 percent to 50 percent of its calories from fat, but most of it is polyunsaturated, which isn't as harmful as the saturated fat found in animal products. In addition, tofu is rarely eaten alone, so when the other ingredients in a particular recipe are taken into account, the percentage of calories from fat in the entire dish will drop.

But don't pick up a block of tofu and dig in with your spoon just yet. Tofu is bland and really isn't meant to be eaten alone; it absorbs the flavors it

Types of Tofu

THERE ARE PRIMARILY two types of tofu: the type packed in tubs of water and refrigerated, or aseptically sealed (packed in cardboard) without water or the necessity for refrigeration. You can also find dried tofu and other kinds in Asian markets. That little jiggling package is packed in three different degrees of firmness. Go ahead and squeeze. Here's a handy little guide for your first forays into tofu:

Silken and Soft. Ideal for blending into creamy salad dressings or for making sauces, dips, custards, and toppings for casseroles.

Medium. Good for puddings, pies, cheesecakes, chunky salads, and fillings of all kinds.

Firm and Extra-Firm. Use for grilling, broiling, stir-frying, "steaks," and kebabs.

comes into contact with. Nearly anything can be used to flavor tofu: ginger, garlic, toasted sesame oil, fragrant broths, and marinades are just a few suggestions. From there, the tofu can be grilled, barbecued, broiled, stir-fried, or scrambled the way you would an egg. It is also great in some puddings and desserts, like chocolate pie. For more hints and recipes on how to use tofu, see Chapter 3.

Tempeh

Tempeh (TEM-pay) is a fermented soybean cake with a nutty aroma and a chewy texture that may remind you of meat. To make tempeh, split and hulled soybeans are inoculated with tempeh starter and fermented in much the same way as cheese. The enzyme action of the starter makes the soybeans easy to digest, while the filaments that form to bind the beans into a cake provide texture and many valuable B vitamins.

Tempeh can be purchased in the frozen-food section of most natural food stores and some supermarkets. There are also ready-made tempeh-based products, including burgers, bacon, and even sloppy joes. Tempeh, like tofu, is also very versatile; try it marinated and then grilled, fried or steamed, or as a meat replacement in stir-fries and casseroles.

Seitan

This chewy food is made from wheat dough that has been kneaded under water to isolate the gluten and wash away the starch and bran. Seitan is very high in protein, and low in fat and calories. It is available jarred, frozen, or fresh. Cut it into strips or cubes for sandwiches, soups, stews, or stir-fries.

TVP (Textured Vegetable Protein)

After soy oil has been extracted from cooked soybeans, defatted soy flakes, which are about 50 percent protein by weight, are left behind. These flakes are put through various acid, base, and alcohol solutions to reduce their carbohydrate content, then further reduced to produce a fiber-spun carbohydrate-free extrusion better known as TVP.

TVP is used to simulate products like burgers and sausage. It's frequently used as one of the ingredients in vegetarian convenience foods such as dry mixes and frozen foods. It's also available plain in granules and chunks for home use in dishes like chili, or flavored in granules, chunks, and slices.

Roasted Soynuts

If you're nuts about roasted peanuts, you'll love this nutritious alternative. Soak soybeans overnight in cold water. The next day, drain the soybeans well and spread on a lightly oiled baking sheet. Roast in a 300°F for thirty to thirty-five minutes, stirring now and then to avoid scorching. Remove from the oven and sprinkle with a little salt, if desired, or a few drops of tamari sauce. Soynuts are also produced commercially and are available in many natural food stores.

Soy Yogurt, Soy Cheese

Soy yogurt is cultured from rich soymilk using active cultures. Creamy and delicious, it has the soy advantages of being lactose and cholesterol-free. Soy cheese is made in both soft and hard varieties. The soft cheese is made from gently aged tofu that is whipped to a creamy consistency, resulting in a product similar to cream cheese. Firm soy cheese is similar to mozzarella in both taste and texture. Both types commonly employ the milk protein casein to hold them together and make them melt, so many vegans do not use them.

A Little Light Reading

As of May 1994, the federal government required all manufacturers to comply with the Nutrition Labeling and Education Act (NLEA), probably better known to you as the "Nutrition Facts" labels on everything from soup to nuts. This legislation came as a result of a government initiative to standardize labeling of all food products and create definitions for popular food buzzwords we see on many packages. Packages too small to hold the nutrition information must provide a toll-free (800) number where it can be obtained.

Many of us don't read these labels because we're unsure of what all the terms and numbers mean, or we really don't want to know how bad the whole bag of potato chips we just scarfed down is for us. But read and used correctly, the new labels provide you an opportunity to know what you're putting into your body and how to manage it better. Try to get into the habit of reading labels to make sure that calories, fat, and cholesterol levels are within your limits.

EVEN THOUGH some products seem vegetarian, they have animal products lurking in them:

- *Gelatin*—made from processed animal bones
- *Marshmallows*—most are made with gelatin
- *Fried foods*—restaurants and some packaged-foods producers fry in lard
- *Desserts with creme filling*—may contain animal fat
- *Dried and canned vegetable soups*—may include dehydrated chicken, pork, or beef broth
- *Canned beans*—may contain chicken, pork, or beef broth

The immediate effects of the labeling are evident just by looking at your grocery store shelves. Part of the labeling initiative included standardizing definitions of what terms such as "lite" and "low-fat" meant, meaning that some manufacturers who were making those claims about their products are now unable to do so. Now, when we see that a product says it is low in fat, we know that it must meet a standard set by the government. Manufacturers whose products still meet these requirements are playing up these advantages on their products and are forever rushing to bring us more healthful products.

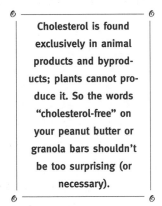

Cholesterol is found exclusively in animal products and byproducts; plants cannot produce it. So the words "cholesterol-free" on your peanut butter or granola bars shouldn't be too surprising (or necessary).

The Nutrition Facts labels come complete with calories per serving, the percentage of calories from fat, and how much fat, cholesterol, and sodium are contained in a serving. Based on a 2,000-calorie-a-day diet, they can be a real boon to the health-conscious, since they're computed on realistic servings rather than those which make the product look good. To help you decipher what you're reading, we have included information that defines the terms most commonly used on the Nutrition Facts labels (see pages 39–40).

The new labels also make it easier for vegetarians to check whether the product contains meat or meat by-products such as animal fat or meat-based broth. If you want to stick to being a true vegetarian, you'll have to make special note of all the ingredients in the foods you buy. Just because a can of soup says "Vegetable Soup" on it doesn't mean it was made without chicken or beef broth.

Deciphering Labeling Terms

If the alphabet soup that appears on your can of vegetable soup is getting you down, use this rundown of common labeling terms so you can make the best food choices for you and your family:

FAT-FREE products may still contain negligible amounts of fat (less than 0.5 grams of fat per serving).

LIGHT or LITE means the food contains one-third fewer calories, one-half the fat compared to the original version or a comparable product.

LOW-FAT food can have up to three grams of fat per serving.

LOW IN SATURATED FAT foods contain one gram or less of saturated fat per serving, with no more than 15 percent of calories coming from saturated fat.

SERVING SIZES. In order to make foods seem better for you than they actually were, manufacturers would shrink their serving sizes to reduce the amount of fat, sodium, cholesterol, and the like. For example, a can of soda used to be listed as two servings. With the new labeling requirements, now each can is a realistic one serving. Product sizes are standardized, making it possible to compare products and their nutritional values with comparable products.

CALORIES FROM FAT, FAT GRAMS, SATURATED FAT. Calories from fat per serving, total grams of fat, and total grams of saturated fat per serving are noted. To figure your percentage of calories from fat, divide the number of calories from fat by the total number of calories in the food, and multiply by 100. For instance, if a 200-calorie food gets fifty of its calories from fat, fifty divided by 200 times 100 equals twenty-five, or 25 percent of calories from fat. All are important, especially the amount of saturated, or "bad," fat. As mentioned previously, foods that are especially high in saturated fat are best avoided.

% DAILY VALUE. Based on 2,000 calories a day, this tells you what percentage of the substance the product contains.

SODIUM. A certain amount of salt is required for a balanced diet, yet salt is a concern to most of us because it is linked to high blood pressure. Try to avoid highly processed foods, which often have large amounts of salt, which is often used as a preservative. Salt-free products have less than five grams per serving; very low sodium, less than thirty-five grams per serving; and low sodium, less than 140 grams of sodium per serving.

TOTAL CARBOHYDRATES. It's recommended that you make complex carbohydrates approximately three-fourths of your diet. This figure tells you how many grams of carbohydrates there are in each serving and how much of the daily requirement this translates to.

PROTEIN. Total grams per serving are noted. Generally speaking, a thirty-year-old male needs about sixty-three grams of protein, while a woman of the same age needs about fifty grams on an average day.

NUTRIENTS. Listed are percentages present in the food or beverage of the four nutrients thought to be most often lacking in the American diet: vitamin A, vitamin C, calcium, and iron. A star after one of these nutrients usually means that the food contains less than 2 percent of the recommended dietary allowance for that nutrient.

INGREDIENTS. A list of what the product contains starts with the most prevalent ingredient and continues to the least dominant. When reading ingredient lists, use common sense: Do you recognize what most of the ingredients are, or do you feel like you're participating in some kind of cruel spelling bee? Try to stick to foods that have ingredients you know. In addition, vegetarians sometimes have to take special note of hidden animal products in certain foods that appear in other incarnations. For example, dairy can be present in a seemingly vegan product in the form of casein, or milk protein, while products that contain Worcestershire sauce may not be vegetarian, because most Worcestershire sauce is made from anchovies.

Riding the Nutrition Roller Coaster

WE'RE FAIRLY CERTAIN THAT this isn't the first book you've consulted when it comes to health. And we're just as certain that it won't be the last. By this time, you've probably figured out that what you eat may eventually come back to

haunt you. What you're probably a bit unsure of is exactly what to believe, based on the many conflicting studies and news reports that you've been bombarded with over the years. The problem is never a lack of information. It is that the information we're getting is in a constant state of flux. Take coffee, for instance. Over the years, we've been told that it's bad for us, then not so bad, then even worse than it was originally supposed to be. It's enough to make anyone head back to the coffee machine for an extra cup out of spite.

It seems like nothing health-related has a shelf life of more than a year. There is always a better way, a radical miracle cure waiting in the wings to make us feel and look healthier than we have ever been before. If you've grown up being taught that certain foods are good for us, many things that we're saying may sound a bit daunting and disconcerting.

This media overload may seem like the perfect excuse not to give up meat, but there's really much more to the story. While a meat-based diet has fluctuated in both support and popularity over the years (with support now on a decline), vegetarians have followed a path that slowly and steadily wins the race. By keeping things simple, which vegetarianism does, you reduce the risk of putting unknown substances into your body that may wind up being found harmful a few years down the road. Over the years, we have begun to learn more about human nutrition and how foods affect our bodies. The passage of time will only yield more knowledge. And as we have learned more, we have found more and more advantages to a vegetarian lifestyle. Vegetarianism is not just the latest fad. It has been around for thousands of years and will be around for thousands more. And as time has told, more and more people have begun to realize that when things get complicated, going back to basics may be the safest and best idea of them all.

☆ne a ᗪay, or ℕone a ᗪay?

PEOPLE HAVE BEEN PONDERING the value of vitamin supplements for years, and today it's still a hot topic in any discussion about nutrition. And after all the news reports, studies, and claims, all we can safely say about supplements is that they are exactly what their name implies. They aren't intended to replace foods, but merely to act as an adjunct to them. Hype aside, vitamins cannot and will not deliver the same range of nutrients and calories as food or make up for excesses in your diets. Eating a balanced diet is the best way to ensure that you will have a long, happy, and healthful life. In other words, don't expect vitamins to compensate for a diet of Twinkies, pretzels, and soda.

Still, the fact remains that some people feel more comfortable adding a multivitamin or other supplement. There really isn't anything wrong with this, provided that moderation and common sense are employed when doing so. (There are thirteen vitamins, nine of them water soluble and four of them fat soluble. Vitamins A, D, and E can accumulate in body fat and reach toxic levels if taken in excessive amounts.) No matter what vitamin you are taking, be sure not to overdo it. Claims that excessive amounts of any vitamin lead to improved performance or feeling may not be all they're cracked up to be.

Without supplements, the only vitamin that vegans may not get through their daily diet is B_{12}, or cobalamin, which assists in both cell and blood development. B_{12} is found only in animal products, but vegetarians really need not worry; B_{12} deficiencies are very rare. This is because if you ever were a meat eater, your body has stored up a supply of B_{12} that some researchers believe can last from five to thirty years. Because of differing scientific opinions on whether the body manufactures B_{12} and whether vegans need a supplement, play it safe by taking a B$_{12}$ supplement or eating a B$_{12}$-fortified cereal a couple of times per week. Another option is to add nutritional yeast to your food; one to two teaspoons contains a week's dietary requirement of the vitamin. Check the package to make sure it supplies B$_{12}$.

There have been stories upon stories filled with evidence published in both medical journals and the lay press linking specific vitamins to better health. This may or may not be true, but if in your case getting a variety of foods every day is difficult, don't throw up your hands. Work harder on your diet by regularly trying and including new and different foods; supplements will never substitute for that.

Nutrition in a Nutshell

TAKE A DEEP BREATH, sit back, and relax. You've finished with the nutrition chapter, and have quite a bit of new information to consider. Before you move on and start trying some of the recipes, we'll try to condense everything we've said here into some simple terms so you know exactly what to do to ensure you're getting a good, solid vegetarian diet. The bottom line is that it isn't that difficult: Your diet should be a celebration of breads and grains, with vegetables and fruits added to provide nutrients, color, texture, and overall interest. From there, what you eat is all up to you.

Your body is sort of like a computer. If you enter the correct commands into it, it will produce what you're looking for. If you eat a poor diet, you'll get sick or, at the very least, will not feel your best. If you put energy-filled carbohydrates into your body, you'll end up feeling lively, healthy, and happy. If you put in fruits and vegetables that are chock-full of vitamins and minerals, your body will be in fine working order, no matter what the rumor mill might say. Protein is not a concern. Iron is not a concern nor is calcium, provided you follow a few simple rules.

Your parents may have taught you to be moderate in all things; to stay slow and steady. You may not have agreed with everything your parents said, but it does turn out that this kernel of wisdom is one of the key rules for living a healthy vegetarian lifestyle. A glass of wine with dinner won't kill you. A scoop of ice cream or frozen yogurt once in a while after a meal is quite a refreshing way to end some quality time with your family. Even nutrition experts like Dean Ornish, M.D., who advocates an extremely low-fat diet (10 percent or less calories from fat) in his best-selling book, *Eat More, Weigh Less*, admits to indulging occasionally in Häagen-Dazs. Like Dr. Ornish, find a way to treat yourself once in a while.

Keep the amount of salt, refined sugar, and fat to a minimum. Don't overcompensate for meat by indulging in dairy products; you'll probably feel no better and, if you're considering vegetarianism for weight loss, you won't achieve your goal because of the high fat content. Finally, read nutrition labels and become a student of what you're eating. With all of these tips, you'll know exactly what to put into your body to make it give you back exactly what you need.

Start with grains, preferably whole grains and the pastas and breads made from them. They're easy to digest and loaded with complex carbohydrates, the body's most readily available source of sustained energy. And ounce for ounce, you'll find the greatest nutritional return. Keep the "demons" of protein, iron, and calcium deficiencies away by doing what you normally do, making sure you're getting plenty of variety. Five servings of vegetables and fruits on a daily basis should do just fine.

When it comes right down to it, vegetarianism is about common sense, not denial. It's about eating a variety of wholesome foods in sufficient quantity to satisfy you, and most experts would agree that it's not necessary to keep track of every fat gram in every meal or even in every day. Mainstream America has finally caught up with the uncomplicated idea of good health through good food. We no longer have to search for special stores to find the foods we need. We can see more clearly than ever before which foods to eat and which to avoid. We've become more savvy about things like additives and preservatives, and about the importance of supplementing our health with exercise.

If there is one thing we can stress once again before moving on, it is one more word about junk food. If that's the way you eat, becoming a vegetarian won't change your health profile very much. Nutritionally, there's not a lot of difference between a vegetarian junk-food diet and a meat-based one. There is, however, a world of difference between a standard American meat-based diet and a standard wholesome vegetarian diet. If you want a healthier future, you have the tools to do it. Now all it takes is a trip to the grocery store, and a promise to make a new start. It's all enjoyment from here.

Further Reading

Diet for a New America, by John Robbins (Stillpoint Publishing, 1987).

Diet for a Small Planet (20th Anniversary Edition), by Frances Moore Lappé (Ballantine Books, 1991).

The Nutrition Debate: Sorting Out Some Answers, by Joan Dye Gussow and Paul R. Thomas, eds. (Bull Publishing, 1986).

Nourishing Wisdom: A New Understanding of Eating, by Marc David (Random House, 1994).

Food and Healing, by Annemarie Colbin (Ballantine Books, 1986).

Ready, Set, Eat!

BEING A VEGETARIAN MEANS YOU HAVE TWO BASIC DIETARY OPTIONS: A
FASCINATING AND NEVER-ENDING VARIETY OF GRAINS, VEGGIES, LEGUMES, AND FRUITS—
OR CANDY BARS, PEANUT BUTTER AND JELLY SANDWICHES, AND POTATO CHIPS.
ADVANTAGES OF THE FIRST OPTION ARE EVIDENT. YOUR HEALTH WILL TAKE A TURN
FOR THE BETTER, YOU'LL LOOK BETTER, AND YOU'LL GET THAT SMUG LITTLE FEELING
OF NUTRITIONAL SUPERIORITY WHEN YOU PASS BY THE MEAT SECTION AT THE
SUPERMARKET. YOU MAY ALSO GET TO HOLD OFF ON THAT MUCH ANTICIPATED
TRIPLE BYPASS FOR A WHILE.

THE ADVANTAGE OF THE SECOND OPTION IS THAT YOU'LL HAVE VERY LITTLE CONTACT
WITH YOUR KITCHEN AGAIN, SOMETHING THAT IS QUITE APPEALING TO THOSE WHO MAY
NOT REMEMBER EXACTLY WHERE THEIR KITCHEN IS LOCATED. ON THE OTHER HAND,
YOU'LL LIKELY GAIN A POUND A DAY AND STILL GET A SHOT AT THAT BYPASS.
IF YOU CHOSE THE SECOND OPTION, SAY HELLO TO A LIFE OF SNICKERS AND SKIPPY.
BUT IF THE FIRST OPTION SOUNDED A BIT BETTER, YOU MAY WANT TO READ ON.

It's Showtime!

SO THIS IS IT. You've told all the significant people in your life that you want to be a vegetarian. Your mother sighed and said it's just another phase. Your friends nodded and gave each other a knowing glance. They're probably dying to remind you about the times you took up break dancing and skydiving.

But a few of your friends believe you're actually serious and have promised to be supportive; maybe they've also expressed some interest in vegetarianism. You've read Chapter 2 and have learned and memorized the many advantages to eliminating meat from your diet, and you've promised everyone that vegetarian food isn't going to be boring or bland. So stop talking about it—it's time to put up or shut up.

Easy Does It

After preparing only a few meatless meals, you're sure to find out that vegetarian cooking is not only good for you; it's easy, flexible, and delicious. In fact, the range of foods and combinations is so vast that you may not have enough years left to explore all the possibilities. The sooner you get started, the more wonderful, healthful food you'll get to experience.

Changing your diet for the better is easier than you may think. Follow your own timetable; there's no reason why you can't make a gradual adjustment to a meatless diet. Start by deciding meal by meal if you want to eat vegetarian, then move to an entire meatless day, then build to two days, and so on. Cut out red meat first and, when you feel ready, stop chicken, turkey, and other poultry. From there, fish and shellfish should be a breeze.

If you find yourself feeling hungry for meat, chicken, or fish, don't beat yourself up over it; there are plenty of meatless alternatives to see you through. The desire to suffer voluntarily is a prerequisite for monkdom, not for being a vegetarian. This isn't a new religion—just a more healthful approach to how you eat and live.

Vegetarian Food? Them's Fightin' Words!

You're probably already familiar with many basic meatless dishes; it's just that nobody ever dared call them vegetarian to your face. Die-hard meat eaters

would probably be shocked to know that even they have had a vegetarian dish from time to time, cleverly disguised with names like eggplant Parmesan, spaghetti, quiche, ratatouille, pasta with pesto sauce, pizza, and a whole lot more. They may even admit to having enjoyed them.

Many people shy away from vegetarianism because they think the food is going to be brown, foreign, and bland. But who doesn't know and love pizza? Or pasta? Or tacos? Not every vegetarian entrée displays every color of the rainbow, but neither does a charred steak or a rack of grilled ribs. The truth about vegetarian food is that it is a combination of adapted old favorites and some new creations made with things that may be a little foreign to you. But there's no harm in giving them a try. You may feel a bit overcome when you step into your first health food store and try to distinguish between bulgur and quinoa, and you may feel a bit uncertain when you first experiment with tofu, tempeh, or seitan. These are reactions that are all normal and will all fade, especially when you find that eating vegetarian is helping you to live a little in more ways than one.

Vegetarians have worked long and hard to discard old stereotypical labels by using two logical arguments—good nutrition and good food. You've got the nutrition part; now you need to learn how to cook meatless dishes that will please even the biggest nonbelievers. The first steps toward doing that are a bit of advance planning and a shopping trip to stock a vegetarian pantry.

Building Your Veg Pantry

TO BE ABLE TO experiment with a wide range of vegetarian recipes, it helps to get yourself an arsenal of food together in advance. What we're suggesting is just that—a suggestion. Feel free to add or delete particular items as you feel you will or won't use them. More than likely, as you begin to feel more comfortable with cooking vegetarian meals, you'll want to broaden your horizons. At one time or another, all of these items should come in handy.

> If you're trying to cut fat and calories in your cooking, good-quality nonstick cookware is a great investment. Nonstick surfaces reduce or eliminate the need for oil or fat in stovetop cooking.

The bottom line of shopping smart really boils down to common sense. Buy the kinds of foods that reflect your lifestyle and food preferences, and buy the best quality you can afford. Don't compromise. For the best produce, buy from local gardens, roadside stands, or farmers' markets whenever possible. Take advantage of whatever is in season because when winter comes, you'll have no choice but to buy produce shipped in from elsewhere.

And even if everything looks fabulous at the farmers' market, keep a limit on what you purchase. If you allow your eyes to be bigger than your needs, you could find yourself staring at rotting vegetables and herbs that may be ready to get up and toss themselves into the garbage. Use the rotation principle to keep your vegetables fresh—first bought is always first used.

Finally, take the time to acquaint yourself with your local natural foods store, where many of the recommended pantry items can be found easily. No, you won't have to walk through beaded doorways, fighting your way through a smoky haze to get to the foods. New upscale mass-market and local natural food stores (Fresh Fields and Bread & Circus) are popping up all over. If you haven't been in a health-food store before, it may seem a bit daunting at first, and many things may be foreign to you, but the natural food store is in many cases the best friend of the vegetarian. Take some time to poke around. You'll soon learn of more healthful variations on traditional foods than you ever thought possible.

The Basic Vegetarian Pantry

TO MAKE THINGS EASIER on your first vegetarian shopping trip, we've put together a handy list. Assemble this cast of characters, and you'll be more than ready to cook healthfully.

Breads and Grains

Regular or quick-cooking brown rice

Oatmeal (one-minute is OK; instant is not)

Whole grain breads (keep an extra loaf or two in the freezer)

Whole grain ready-to-eat cereal (without added salt and sugar)

Whole grain crackers (without added salt and sugar)

Whole grain pastas (also look for Asian rice and buckwheat noodles)

Egg Replacer (a combination of starches and leavening agents that binds and leavens in cooked and baked foods)

Fruits and Vegetables

Canned whole Italian plum tomatoes

Canned stewed tomatoes

Canned artichoke hearts

Fresh produce: Apples, oranges, lemons, onions (red and yellow), garlic, carrots, celery, cilantro or parsley, russet baking potatoes, waxy thin-skinned potatoes for boiling

---

In choosing fruit to be cooked, you don't have to be as finicky as you would be if you were going to eat it raw. Bruised fruit is fine as long as the bruise is not a symptom of decay. Cut away the soft spot before adding the fruit to the dish.

Ripeness *is* important for adequate flavor. To determine whether fruit is ripe, smell it. If the peaches, plums, or pineapples smell like peaches, plums, or pineapples, chances are they're ripe. If their aroma is weak, they may be underripe and their flavor may be bland. If they smell cloying, tinny, or just plain bad, pass them by.

Fruits and Vegetables (*continued*)

Frozen vegetables and fruits: Spinach, broccoli, tiny peas, mixed vegetables, baby lima beans, corn, green beans, peaches, strawberries, raspberries

Nuts, Seeds, and Beans

Canned and/or dried beans: White, northern, navy, black, chickpeas (garbanzos), red (Mexican or kidney), pinto, black-eyed peas

Natural peanut butter (no added sugar or salt)

Tahini (sesame paste)

Tofu: Water-packed firm and/or extra-firm water-packed, aseptically packed silken

Unsalted nuts: Walnuts, pecans, pine nuts

Eggs and Dairy Products

Eggs (organic, free-range, or egg substitute)

Reduced or fat-free dairy cheeses or soy cheeses: Mozzarella, cheddar, cream cheese

Low or fat-free cottage cheese

Low-fat or nonfat yogurt

Soymilk or skim milk

Soy or unhydrogenated margarine

Condiments, Thickeners, and Seasonings

Agar-agar for thickening and as a gelatin substitute (gelatin is an animal product)

Arrowroot or cornstarch

Vegetarian bouillon granules or cubes, or canned vegetable broth

Basic seasonings: Cinnamon, coarse kosher or sea salt, peppercorns, cayenne pepper, dried red pepper flakes, dry mustard, paprika, chili powder, cumin, thyme, basil, oregano, rosemary, marjoram, garlic powder, fresh ginger root

Tabasco or other hot pepper sauce

Tamari or low-sodium soy sauce

Condiments, Thickeners, and Seasonings (*continued*)

Maple syrup

Molasses

Olive oil

Canola oil

Nonstick vegetable spray

Salsa, jarred

Tomato paste

Tomato sauce

Unsweetened apple or other fruit butter and fruit conserves

Red wine vinegar

Apple cider vinegar

Rice vinegar

Beverages

Fruit and vegetable juices: Apple, tomato, V-8

Leaf and herbal teas

Organic coffee or cereal-grain beverages

Sparkling water

Balance Is Beautiful

IF YOU SHOPPED TILL you dropped, and your pantry is so full of good food that it wants to rip its doors off and cook a meal for you, you're ready for the next steps on your way to a wonderful meal. It's always best to know in advance what you're striving for, and then move on to the finer points of exactly how to get from A to B. Questions fill your mind. What exactly makes up a good vegetarian meal? What are the best ways to prepare it? It all begins with balance.

There's a myth floating around that a balanced vegetarian diet is nothing more than the typical American diet without meat. Well, it could be just the

Veggie Etiquette

TAKE GOOD CARE of the fruits and vegetables you buy, and they'll take care of you. Wash them, and separate root vegetables from their green tops, leaving about an inch still attached. If they came from a roadside stand or farmers' market, they may need a little more trimming than those purchased from a supermarket. Wrap the greens in paper or cloth towels or place them in a perforated plastic vegetable bag. Refrigerate everything on the lowest shelf of your refrigerator, but store tomatoes at room temperature, not in the refrigerator. Cold destroys both their taste and texture.

If you've never tasted the tender tops of young carrots and beets steamed and lightly seasoned, you're in for a treat. The root ends won't need to be wrapped, especially if you plan to use them within a day or two; store them as soon as possible after purchasing.

baked potato and mixed green salad that used to go along with that old piece of steak, but it sure would be dull, and vegetarian eating is anything but boring. A vegetarian meal is considered balanced when it provides the right nutrients in the right amounts and is a joy for both the eyes and the taste buds.

You really don't have to be a scientist to get everything you need from your meatless diet. The foundation begins with either a whole grain, a whole grain pasta, or a whole grain bread. Whole grains are full of the complex carbohydrates, protein, iron, and many other necessary minerals your body needs every day. Ideally, various carbohydrate sources will constitute about three-quarters of your daily diet while accounting for about half of your daily calorie intake. You'll want to avoid refined grains, which are much lower in nutrients due to the removal of the bran and germ during the refining process.

Vegetables and fruits are your next major building block toward a balanced diet. Not only are they rich in carbohydrates, vitamins (particularly A and C), minerals, and fiber, they add color and flavor to a multitude of grain-based dishes. Five servings of vegetables or fruits a day is a good goal; there is always a wide variety of produce in season, so you'll never have to search too long for something that suits you. Remember, when you cook

A Hill of Beans

A DRIED BEAN may look just like any other dried bean, but if it was dried a year or more ago, it may never cook tender again. Year-old dried chickpeas (garbanzos), for example, have been known to take up to six hours of cooking after overnight soaking. The only exceptions to this rule are split peas and lentils.

Be sure to rinse and pick over dried agricultural products such as beans, lentils, and barley. They may contain dirt and small bits of gravel missed in the packaging process.

If you buy your beans where turnover is fairly rapid, they can be tender and ready to use in between one and two hours. If they are sold in bulk, so much the better, because you can buy exactly what you need when you need it. Try to buy dried beans at a natural food store if possible since supermarkets buy in huge lots, and thus the beans may be too old. Protect dried beans and grains from mold and/or infestation by storing them in airtight containers with a bay leaf buried in the middle.

vegetables, avoid butter or margarine, which can easily make something that is nutritious not so.

If you're wondering how you can possibly get the right amounts of protein, calcium, and iron without using animal products, the solution can once again be found in grains and vegetables. Peas, beans, tofu, tempeh, nuts, and seeds all contain more than enough protein; calcium is abundant in broccoli, turnip greens, figs, soybeans, and acorn squash; and whole grains, broccoli, leafy greens, and other vegetables are all rich in iron. If you eat these foods daily, you'll be getting a balanced, complete diet with the added advantage of not having to process all the fatty baggage that comes with consuming animal products that are high in these nutrients.

The little things also make a meal memorable, such as the texture and appearance of food combinations. Take a bite of creamy-smooth mashed potatoes with crunchy onion bits hidden in the middle and you'll know what we mean. Feast your eyes upon a pale golden pasta laced with basil leaves and sun-dried tomatoes—something that is as good to look at as it is to eat. All you have to do is add a simple steamed vegetable or side salad, some whole grain bread, and dessert to bring the meal into perfect balance.

Another good technique is playing rich dishes off of light ones by alternating them. If you start out with a thick, hearty soup, switch to something like a mixed salad afterward. You could also make the soup a light Asian-style broth, followed by a sturdy stick-to-the-ribs kind of stew or casserole with slabs of whole grain bread, and wind up with fresh fruit.

Cook to Win

YOU MUST BE GETTING impatient (and hungry) because you still haven't eaten, but we still have to show you how to prepare this wonderful stuff! This lesson should be pretty short, because all in all, the predominant cooking techniques for vegetables are exactly the same you used before, with some minor variations. If you already know how to stir-fry, braise, steam, broil, and sauté, you're ready to prepare a vegetarian meal. Even charcoal grilling, historically the reserve of summertime steaks and burgers, is a wonderful way to cook vegetables, and veggie burgers and hot dogs.

Microwaving vegetables is easy and healthful. The microwave's effect of locking in vitamins is similar to that of steaming. Very little water is needed and, as with steaming, cooking times vary (usually no more than three minutes) according to size and type of vegetable.

The goal when cooking vegetables is to tenderize the texture of the food without sacrificing its color, flavor, or nutrients. Choose the appropriate technique for the vegetable, and success (and finally, a meal!) will be yours.

No matter what cooking technique you use, you'll want to taste everything before taking it off of the heat. As soon as the vegetables feel tender to your teeth, yet have a little resistance left, you've got it.

DEEP BATH BOILING. This is an especially good way to cook carrots, beets, potatoes, and various other green vegetables. It is a quick and efficient way to achieve good texture, color, and flavor.

Fill a large pot with enough water so the vegetables can roll around freely once the water begins boiling. Add salt (if desired) and bring the water to a full boil. Drop the vegetables in gradually so that the water continues to boil. Begin timing, but do not cover the pot. Remember to always cut vegetables into uniformly sized pieces so they will cook in the same amount of time. Onion, garlic, herbs, and spices will all add flavor through the cooking water. When the vegetables are tender, scoop them out with a slotted spoon and you're ready to go.

STEAMING. In this method, vegetables steam in the water vapor instead of the water itself, in a way that doctors and nutritionists consider to be the best method for preserving vegetable nutrients. Collapsible stainless steel steamers and bamboo racks are inexpensive and easy to find, or you can improvise with a metal colander or wire rack set into a large pan. The newer electric countertop steamers with built-in timers are a bit more expensive but very handy. Almost all vegetables steam well, particularly tender ones like leafy greens or snow peas.

Boil a pot of water, keeping the water level just below the steaming tray. Place the vegetables on the tray. For even results, arrange vegetables in a single layer and avoid overfilling the pan. Cover the pot and reduce the heat to medium. It's important not to allow the water to boil away. The timing is similar to that for deep bath boiling: Tender vegetables take one to three minutes; sturdy ones need more time.

BRAISING AND STEWING. When you slowly simmer a single vegetable in a small amount of stock or liquid, you're braising. Stewing is closely related, with the exception that several differently flavored vegetables are cooked at once in more liquid that is not completely boiled away.

To braise, start cooking using a medium saucepan with a little seasoning and enough water to come halfway up the sides of the food. Cover and cook over medium heat until almost tender, then uncover, raise the heat, and rapidly boil the liquid away, leaving only about a tablespoon of syrupy liquid clinging to the vegetable. If you're stewing, fill the pot almost to the top with water and follow the directions for braising. However, at the end, do not raise the temperature to boil the liquid away.

> Cooking with parchment paper (available in most grocery stores) is another easy and healthful way to cook, offering the combined benefits of steaming and baking. Try sealing different combinations of herbs and vegetables with a small amount of cooking liquid in parchment and placing it in the oven for ten to twenty minutes. The flavors will mingle without any oil. Serve the dish directly from the paper packet, and there is virtually no cleanup!

SAUTÉING. When you sauté, you're tossing vegetables around in an uncovered pan heated to high temperatures. Any skillet can be used to sauté, although a larger one is preferred to allow more room for the ingredients. Use a tiny amount of oil or a liquid such as water, wine, or stock (no more than a quarter of a cup for a large skillet) to begin. Maintaining a high temperature, add dry, uniformly cut vegetables slowly in order to avoid reducing the heat. If you crowd the pan, the ingredients will steam instead of sauté. Shake the pan often or stir continuously with a spatula until vegetables are crisp-tender.

When more than one kind of vegetable is involved, start with the longest-cooking first and work gradually toward the fastest-cooking. Diagonally cut slices have a greater surface area, which speeds the cooking process and helps vegetables absorb more of the seasonings.

STIR-FRYING. This is sautéing, Asian-style. High heat and brief cooking are the keys here, and although a well-seasoned wok is preferred, you can also

Triumphing over Tofu

YOU KNOW IT'S a terrific meat substitute. You know it's good for you. You know it can be one of the most versatile foods known to man. And there it sits on your counter, mysteriously jiggling around in its plastic package. Don't be afraid—free yourself from tofu phobia and take the needed steps to send you on your way to a taste sensation. Cut extra-firm tofu into chunks or triangles and it becomes a good substitute for chicken or beef in stir-fry dishes. Add tiny cubes of it to clear soups for texture. Whip it with a few herbs for a creamy low calorie salad dressing or combine it with crunchy vegetables to make a smooth dip.

To cook tofu, you must first press it to remove excess moisture. Here's how: Cut drained, water-packed extra-firm tofu into one-inch slices. Place the slices on a tray or plate lined with a thick cloth towel or several layers of paper towels. Cover the slices with more towels, then place a plate or board on top. Add weights (such as one-pound cans) and allow the tofu to rest undis- turbed. After twenty or thirty minutes, the tofu slices will be relatively free of moisture and will brown well without sticking. Wrap them well to store in the refrigerator for up to five days.

For a chewy texture similar to meat, freeze tofu first. If the tofu is water packed, you can either freeze it in the container in which it was packed or drain and then freeze it. After a minimum of twenty-four hours in the freezer, thaw the tofu overnight in your refrigerator. Squeeze out excess water with your hands and proceed with the recipe.

use a large heavy skillet. Cut ingredients into a uniform size, then line them up next to the cooking pan in their order of use. Flavoring agents such as garlic and ginger are added first, tofu next, the longest-cooking ingredients (usually carrots and other root vegetables) next, and the shortest-cooking ones (green peas, scallions, etc.) last.

Heat a wok or skillet until very hot. Add a small amount of oil or liquid, and wait about one minute until it begins to bubble; then begin adding the vegetables. Instead of shaking the pan, keep moving the vegetables with a spatula in between adding other ingredients. Serve vegetables immediately to keep a crisp-tender texture.

BROILING AND GRILLING. Broiled or grilled vegetables are cooked by direct radiant heat, which produces a delicious smoky exterior and a tender interior. A perforated enamel rack is a good investment, since regular metal grills are usually too far apart for anything but corn on the cob and whole potatoes. Vegetables can also be skewered to keep them from falling through to the hot coals below. Either way, oil the grill or rack just before cooking.

Light coals thirty to forty-five minutes before you plan to cook. When coals are gray, they're hot enough. A gas grill requires only about five minutes of preheating; an oven broiler between five and ten minutes.

Tomatoes, peppers, eggplant, sweet potatoes, mushrooms, whole scallions or sliced onions, leeks, fennel, summer squash, and even snow peas can be grilled. Slice vegetables about one-half inch thick, or into one-inch cubes for kebabs. Before setting them on the rack, marinate or spray the vegetables lightly with nonstick cooking spray.

Longer-cooking vegetables such as potatoes, winter squashes (including pumpkin), turnips, and rutabagas should be parboiled before grilling. Peel and slice them a half-inch thick, then boil or steam the slices for five minutes. Dry, then spray the vegetables with a little oil before grilling. Lightly oil whole bulbs of garlic, wrap in foil, and place on the side of the grill where coals aren't as hot. Cook thirty to forty-five minutes, or until soft.

If You're on the Fast Track

ALL OF US FIND ourselves running from place to place every once in a while, unable to take the time to cook that brown rice or chop those veggies. But with the host of quick, easy-to-prepare convenience products available, you'll never have to stray from your meatless diet. Dishes like cheese-filled manicotti and ravioli, eggplant parmigiana, vegetable lasagna, and more can all be found at a natural food store or supermarket near you.

You may opt for the convenience of canned beans instead of dried ones. Or you may decide that soaking and cooking beans is worth an hour or two of your time once a week because, once cooked, they can be frozen in meal-size containers and eaten in a jiffy later. If you're really pressed for time, produce is available peeled, washed, and ready to cook. You can even buy salads ready to toss with a dressing.

For you movers and shakers, here is a list of just a few of the foods that save time without forcing you to turn to that Bageldog lurking in the back of your freezer.

If you've ever scrubbed a charred pan after cooking a roast or soaked a grease-laden stockpot, you'll welcome the ease of cleaning a vegetarian kitchen. No more bones or innards to dispose of and no more worrying about salmonella from raw chicken lurking on your cutting board. (For more about food-borne illnesses, see pages 133–34).

CANNED BEANS. Supermarkets and natural food stores carry a wide assortment of canned beans, including organic and with or without salt. Supermarket brands tend to be higher in salt and are sometimes sweetened. Rinse any canned beans in cold water before using, to reduce sodium content.

INSTANT BEANS. A miracle of modern food technology, dried flaked beans produce excellent results, and in only five minutes! You can get instant beans with only salt added or black and refried beans, which include onions, spices, oil, and salt.

CANNED VEGETABLE BROTH AND INSTANT BROTH POWDER. Tasty with herbs and spices, here's a quick and easy way to add flavor and depth to all kinds of vegetarian dishes. Supermarkets offer a variety of meat-free brands, but many contain monosodium glutamate (MSG) and plenty of oil and salt, so check your labels.

PIZZA CRUSTS. Ready-to-use pizza crusts are available in refrigerated, frozen, and fresh versions. Some have cheese and herbs added; others are just flour, water, and maybe a little oil. Why not pop one in the oven with veggies and maybe a little soy cheese on top?

QUICK-COOKING RICE. Gone are the days when brown rice meant forty-five minutes of stovetop cooking. Supermarket brands as well as natural food store brands offer quick-cooking versions of several different rices.

The Most Wonderful Times of the Year?

HOLIDAYS ARE THE times when new vegetarians find themselves remembering, with nostalgia, the old traditional menus, especially the ones that Mom used to make. If you find yourself missing the turkey on Thanksgiving or barbecued hot dogs on the Fourth of July, you should know that with vegetarianism, old habits die more easily than you think.

Don't be surprised if you find your memory more satisfying than reality. After just a few months on a meatless diet, your palate will be cleaner and clearer and you'll find that meat has taken on a heavy, greasy taste. That turkey and ham might smell the same, but they sure won't taste anything like you remember.

So what do you do at holiday time when meat just doesn't taste good anymore or has become otherwise unacceptable? Perhaps the family is coming to your house for Thanksgiving dinner and they're expecting a turkey in the center of the table. Do you cook it or try to explain its absence? And if you can keep crazy meat-eating Uncle Ned from killing and eating you, what do you serve? Here are three suggestions to keep the holidays joyous.

1. Tell them before they come that you want them to try a new kind of holiday meal—one without meat. Then work your hardest to prove how gorgeous and satisfying a meatless meal can be. Consult any one of a wealth of vegetarian cookbooks for some main course ideas, then add a Waldorf salad, some creamed baby lima beans with corn, yams candied in real maple syrup, cabbage slaw, and a homemade pumpkin pie.

2. Prepare the usual holiday dinner including the meat entrée, adding on an extra meatless dish or two for yourself and any other vegetarians who might be at your table. Encourage everyone to try these meatless dishes, and the next time you host a family gathering, they might be happy without the turkey.

3. Take everyone out to a good restaurant and let them order whatever they like. It's not a cop-out to live and let live, provided you are staying true to what you believe in. Not forcing your beliefs on others may convince them to give your way a try another time.

FROZEN FOODS. Yes, the vegetarian TV dinner does exist, along with other old favorites like cheese ravioli, stuffed shells, egg rolls, bean burritos, and pizzas. You can find them at most supermarkets or natural food stores. Be sure to look over the nutritional information

> Freeze leftover rice, pasta, and beans in meal-size portions. They reheat quickly on the stove.

before buying something prohibitively high in fat. Frozen vegetables and fruits are also good quick stand-ins for fresh produce that can usually be cooked in minutes.

KASHA (TOASTED BUCKWHEAT GROATS). Look for this in the kosher foods section of your supermarket. Medium grind is best, with a total cooking time of only fifteen minutes. Buckwheat groats are also available in natural food stores, both toasted and untoasted (white). Buy them already ground for greatest convenience.

COUSCOUS. This semolina-based pasta looks like tiny golden pellets and is ready in only five minutes. Available at both supermarkets and natural food stores, couscous is presteamed and needs no cooking, just a soak in a hot liquid. Toss with steamed or stir-fried vegetables for a nearly instant meal.

Ladies and Gentlemen, Start Your Burners!

SO THERE YOU HAVE IT. Stocked pantry—check. Familiar with the basic cooking methods—check. You're ready, willing, and able to give vegetarian eating a whirl.

To help put theory into practice, we've developed two weeks of menus that are designed to get you thinking in the vegetarian mindset. Why not try a menu or two out this week, beginning the process of gradually replacing meat in your diet with natural foods? From there, the possibilities (and the health benefits) are limitless.

Recipes for Good Health

Menu #1

Fettucine with Black Olive Pesto and Scallions

Tomato and Mozzarella Salad with Vinaigrette

Hot Garlic Bread

Pasta is a vegetarian staple—but that doesn't have to mean eating plain spaghetti with tomato sauce every night. You can easily perk up your pasta with a variety of vegetables, seasonings, and sauces, as we have done in the first menu.

Fettucine with Black Olive Pesto and Scallions

6

makes 4 large servings

1 or 2 fresh jalapeño peppers, seeded and sliced

2 cloves garlic

2 tablespoons chopped onion

2 tablespoons chopped fresh parsley

1 teaspoon fresh thyme, or ½ teaspoon dried thyme

One 9-ounce can pitted black olives (plus 3 tablespoons black olive brine)

1 teaspoon red wine vinegar

1 tablespoon olive oil

10 ounces spaghetti or fettucine

Salt and coarsely ground black pepper to taste

Grated zest of 1 medium lemon

4 large scallions, thinly sliced

1. Set a large pot of lightly salted water on high heat to come to a full rolling boil.

2. In a food processor fitted with a steel blade, finely mince the jalapeños, garlic, and onion. Add parsley, thyme, olives and brine, vinegar, and oil to the garlic mixture; pulse three or four times to coarsely chop olives and combine ingredients. Set aside.

3. Drop fettucine into boiling water and cook rapidly according to package directions until al dente. Set a large colander into a large serving dish and place both in the sink. Pour the pasta into the colander, automatically warming the serving dish while at the same time draining the pasta.

4. Discard cooking water. Dry underside of dish with a towel, and fill it with fettucine. Top with pesto sauce, six to eight grinds of fresh pepper, and salt to taste. Scatter lemon zest and sliced scallions over top.

> To peel a garlic clove, blanch in boiling water for a minute or crush the clove slightly with the flat side of a knife. The skin will practically fall away.

Tomato and Mozzarella Salad with Vinaigrette

—————— 6 ——————

makes 4 servings

4 large or 8 medium plum tomatoes

8 ounces part-skim mozzarella cheese, thinly sliced

6 large fresh basil leaves, thinly sliced

Low-fat vinaigrette or oil and vinegar salad dressing

1. Stand tomatoes, core down, on cutting board, and make vertical ¼-inch-thick slices, stopping just short of the core. Gently press each on the side to open into a fan. Place one large or two small fans on each of 4 salad plates. Slide a slice of cheese between each tomato slice.

2. Scatter basil over each salad, and drizzle with dressing. Serve at once.

Shopping List for Menu #1

Pantry Staples

Garlic, 2 cloves

Salt

Fresh black pepper

Red wine vinegar

Extra-virgin olive oil

Spaghetti or fettucine, 10 ounces

Black olives, pitted, 9-ounce can

Refrigerator/Freezer Staples and Perishables

Low-fat vinaigrette or oil and vinegar dressing

Fresh parsley

Fresh or dried thyme

Scallions, 1 bunch

Fresh basil

Onion, 1 small

Lemon, 1 medium

Jalapeño pepper, 1 or 2

Tomatoes, 4 large or 8 medium plum tomatoes

Mozzarella cheese, 8 ounces

Garlic bread, 1 loaf

Menu #2

Vegetarian Paella

Steamed Sugar Snap Peas

Tomato and Orange Salad

Paella originated in Valencia and originally included chicken, sausage, and shellfish. Ours is an assortment of aromatic and sweet vegetables, including fennel, sweet onion, artichoke hearts, and a bright tangle of red and yellow bell pepper ribbons. Saffron is used for both its color and perfume but, if unavailable, turmeric may be substituted. Lightly steamed sugar snap peas complement this dish perfectly, along with a Spanish-style salad of ripe tomatoes and oranges.

Vegetarian Paella

———— 6 ————

makes 4 large servings

3 tablespoons olive oil

1 medium onion, coarsely chopped

4 cloves garlic, minced

1 fennel bulb, trimmed and thinly sliced; reserve fronds

1 bay leaf

1 ½ cups quick-cooking brown rice

1 large red bell pepper, seeded and cut into thin strips

1 large yellow bell pepper, seeded and cut into thin strips

One 15-ounce can artichoke hearts, drained and quartered

½ cup dry white wine

2 cups "chicken-flavored" vegetable broth, made from granules or canned

Pinch saffron threads or ¼ teaspoon turmeric

Salt and freshly ground black pepper to taste

1. Heat oil in a large heavy paella pan or 2-quart Dutch oven. Add onion; cook, stirring, over moderate heat 1 minute. Add garlic; cook, stirring, 2 minutes. Add fennel and bay leaf; cook 3 minutes, stirring occasionally, until fennel is crisp-tender.

2. Add rice, bell peppers, artichokes, wine, broth, and saffron or turmeric. Add salt and pepper. Raise heat, stir well, and bring to a boil. Cover, and simmer over the lowest possible heat 10 minutes or until liquid has been absorbed. Adjust seasonings if needed.

3. Mince the reserved fennel fronds and sprinkle over paella. Serve at once.

> The next time you buy extra peppers or tomatoes, wash and freeze them whole in plastic bags; thaw and trim if needed. Though not crisp enough for salad, they're perfect for stews, soups, sauces, and entrées, especially in winter when prices are high and good vegetables are hard to find. Frozen tomato skins slide right off without blanching.

Tomato and Orange Salad

———— 6 ————

makes 4 servings

2 Temple or Valencia seedless
   oranges

4 large or 8 small Roma or plum
   tomatoes

1 medium head Boston lettuce

1 medium red onion, peeled, thinly
   sliced, and separated into rings

Reduced-fat salad dressing

1. Peel oranges, and cut them horizontally into $1/4$-inch-thick slices; set aside. Cut tomatoes vertically into quarters. With a small spoon, scoop out core and seeds and discard.

2. Arrange lettuce leaves on 4 salad plates. On each plate arrange 2 or 3 slices of orange, a few onion rings, and 4 pieces of tomato. Drizzle lightly with dressing.

Shopping List for Menu #2

Pantry Staples

Extra-virgin olive oil

Quick-cooking brown rice

Dry white wine

"Chicken-flavored" vegetable broth granules (enough for 2 cups broth), or 2 cans regular vegetable broth

Saffron or turmeric

Bay leaf, 1

Garlic, 4 cloves

Salt

Fresh black pepper

Refrigerator/Freezer Staples and Perishables

Reduced-fat salad dressing

Onion, 1 medium

Fennel bulb with stalks and fronds

Red bell pepper, 1

Yellow bell pepper, 1

Artichoke hearts, 15-ounce can

Frozen sugar snap pea pods, 20-ounce package, or equivalent fresh peas

Temple or Valencia seedless oranges, 2 large

Roma or plum tomatoes, 4 large or 8 small

Red onion, 1 medium

Boston lettuce, 1 medium head

If bell peppers unsettle your stomach, tame them by blanching in boiling water for one minute and plunging them into cold water, which helps to neutralize some of the acids in the peppers. Then proceed with your recipe.

Menu #3

Quick Minestrone

Sun-Dried Tomato, Veggie, and Goat Cheese Pizza

Mixed Greens with Olives

Serve the Quick Minestrone first, then the pizza hot from the oven, and, finally, round out the meal with a simple salad of mixed greens and olives. Double the minestrone recipe to make two meals, if you like; it won't take any more cooking time.

Quick Minestrone

——— 6 ———

makes 4 servings

If you cook often, get in the habit of making stock regularly. Simmer up a batch once a month and freeze it in ice cube trays. When the cubes are frozen, store them in a self-sealing freezer bag, ready to be thawed quickly in whatever amount you need. One cube of broth generally equals a quarter cup once thawed.

1 tablespoon olive oil

1 medium onion, chopped

1 stalk celery with leaves, chopped

1 large clove garlic, minced

2 teaspoons dried Italian herb blend

3 tablespoons raw quick-cooking brown rice

1 large unpeeled potato, cut into ¼-inch dice

10-ounce package frozen mixed vegetables

4 cups canned vegetable broth

One 15-ounce can cannellini or other small white beans, drained and rinsed

⅓ cup elbow or small pasta shells

2 tablespoons tomato paste

Salt and freshly ground pepper to taste

Grated Parmesan cheese for garnish, optional

1. Heat oil in a large saucepan placed over medium-high heat. Add onion, celery, garlic, and Italian herbs. Cook, stirring, until onion is translucent (about 5 minutes) and herbs begin to release their flavor. Add rice, potato, mixed vegetables, and vegetable broth. Cover; simmer 10 minutes.

2. Stir in beans, pasta, and tomato paste. Bring to a boil again over high heat. Reduce heat to low, cover, and simmer 10 minutes or until pasta is al dente. Add salt and pepper. Garnish with Parmesan.

To avoid overcooking frozen vegetables, thaw them first by placing them in a colander, then running water through them until they separate and the ice crystals melt. Cook for 2 ½ minutes—no more!

Sun-Dried Tomato, Veggie, and Goat Cheese Pizza

6

makes 4 servings

3/4 cup oil-packed sun-dried tomatoes, drained and thinly sliced

2 tablespoons oil from sun-dried tomatoes, divided

5 to 6 large basil leaves, thinly sliced

1/4 pound mild goat cheese

10-inch prebaked pizza shell

1 medium onion, halved and thinly sliced

4 ounces large mushrooms, stemmed and thinly sliced

Freshly ground black pepper to taste

1 tablespoon minced fresh rosemary or 1 teaspoon dried rosemary

3 tablespoons grated Parmesan cheese

1. Adjust oven rack to middle position; preheat oven to 400° F.

2. In a small bowl, combine dried tomatoes, half of the tomato oil, basil, and goat cheese. With a spatula, spread the tomato–goat cheese mixture over prebaked pizza shell to within 1 inch of outside edge. Scatter onion and mushrooms over cheese. Grind fresh pepper over all, then scatter with rosemary.

> Mushrooms brown quickly in a damp refrigerator, so store them in a paper bag. It helps draw out accumulated moisture and keeps them white longer.

3. Drizzle remaining oil over pizza; sprinkle with Parmesan. Bake 10 to 15 minutes. Serve at once, cut in wedges.

Mixed Greens with ☆Olives

---- 𝒸 ----

makes 4 servings

½ pound mixed greens, or
 1 package pre-cut salad mix

1 cup sliced green olives stuffed
 with pimiento

1 cup sliced black olives

Freshly ground black pepper

1 tablespoon olive oil

2 to 3 tablespoons brine from
 green olives

1. Arrange mixed greens, green olives, and black olives in a large salad bowl. Grind black pepper over all. Sprinkle with olive oil and green olive brine. Toss well before serving.

Dry, crisp salad is a breeze if you spread freshly washed greens in a layer onto a terrycloth kitchen towel. Roll, tuck in the sides, and place on a lower refrigerator shelf. The towel acts as a wick, first absorbing the water that clings to the greens, then slowly feeding it back as needed.

Shopping List for Menu #3

Pantry Staples

Garlic, 1 large clove

Sun-dried tomatoes, oil packed

Extra-virgin olive oil

Dried Italian herb blend

Quick-cooking brown rice

Potato, 1 large

Vegetable broth, 4 cups

15-ounce can cannellini or other small white beans

Elbow or small-shell pasta

Tomato paste

Salt

Fresh black pepper

Refrigerator/Freezer Staples and Perishables

Grated Parmesan cheese

10-ounce package frozen mixed vegetables

Onions, 2 medium

Celery, 1 stalk

Green olives, 1 cup

Black olives, 1 cup

Prebaked 10-inch pizza crust

Goat cheese, 4 ounces

Mushrooms, 4 ounces

Fresh basil, 1 small bunch

Fresh rosemary, 1 sprig, or dried rosemary

Assorted greens, 1/2 pound, or 1 package pre-cut salad mix

Menu #4

Glazed Root Vegetables

Two-Rice Pilaf with Pecans

Apple Salad

The technique of braising works especially well with winter vegetables where a bit of extra cooking time is needed to fully develop the flavors. Choose your favorite root vegetables, making sure to use carrots for their sweetness.

Glazed Root Vegetables

—————— *6* ——————

makes 4 servings

1 ½ pounds assorted root vegetables (choose three or four from: carrots, rutabaga, celeriac, beets, white turnips, parsnips, russet potato, or small whole onions)

2 tablespoons margarine, divided

1 tablespoon sugar

1 ½ cups water

Salt to taste

1. Trim stem ends from each vegetable; peel and rinse well under cold running water. Cut vegetables into 2-inch chunks; arrange in a single layer in a large heavy nonstick skillet with a cover.

2. Add 1 tablespoon margarine, sugar, and water to come halfway up the sides of vegetables. Cover tightly. Bring to a boil, lower heat, and simmer 15 minutes.

3. Remove lid, raise heat to medium, and continue cooking 10 minutes until liquid is reduced to a thick syrup or glaze. Shake pan to move the vegetables around and keep them from sticking. Turn off heat, add remaining tablespoon margarine, salt to taste, and toss or stir carefully to combine.

Two-Rice Pilaf with Pecans

6

makes 4 servings

1 cup quick-cooking brown rice

²/₃ cup instant wild rice

2 cups vegetable stock or "chicken-flavored" vegetable stock, divided

1 tablespoon canola oil

1 medium onion, halved lengthwise and thinly sliced

¼ cup chopped pecans

Salt and freshly ground black pepper to taste

Finely chopped parsley to taste

1. Cook brown rice and wild rice in separate pans according to package directions, using 1 ¼ cups stock for brown rice and ²/₃ cup of stock for wild rice.

2. While rices cook, heat oil in a medium sauté pan. Add onion and cook, stirring often, until it is translucent and tender, 10 to 15 minutes. Add pecans, brown and wild rices, salt, and pepper. Fold in parsley just before serving.

Save vegetable trimmings and peelings in a large freezer container and make a quick vegetable stock from them. Use the peels and/or leaves of onions, garlic, carrots, celery, turnips, parsnips, parsley stems, and any leftover salad and cooked vegetables. Do not include strongly flavored vegetables such as spinach, asparagus, broccoli, cabbage, and brussels sprouts. Also exclude potatoes, rice, or pasta, as they tend to cloud the stock. Transfer scraps and peelings to a pot. Add water to cover; an extra carrot, onion, and celery for richness; and the seasonings of your choice. Bring to a simmer, cover, and cook 30 minutes. Strain and discard solids, then cool uncovered. Refrigerate or freeze until needed.

Apple Salad

makes 4 servings

½ cup low-fat or fat-free mayonnaise

½ cup sugar-free applesauce

1 to 2 tablespoons honey

1 tablespoon fresh lemon juice

¼ teaspoon salt

3 large Golden Delicious apples

3 stalks celery hearts, cut into ¼-inch dice

½ cup dry-roasted sunflower seeds

½ cup golden seedless raisins

1. In a large bowl, whisk together mayonnaise, applesauce, honey, lemon juice, and salt; set aside.

2. Peel, core, and coarsely dice apples. Toss lightly with dressing. Add diced celery, sunflower seeds, and raisins. May be served room temperature or chilled.

> Lemon juice, wine, or flavored vinegar can enhance taste, eliminating the need for salt. To release more juice from lemons, warm them in a microwave at 50 percent power for 20 seconds before cutting.

Shopping List for Menu #4

Pantry Staples

Canola oil

Golden seedless raisins

Dry-roasted sunflower seeds

Honey

Sugar

"Chicken-flavored" vegetable
broth granules (enough for 2
cups broth), or 2 cans regular
vegetable broth

Quick-cooking brown rice

Instant wild rice

Chopped pecans

Salt

Fresh black pepper

Refrigerator or Freezer Staples

Margarine

Onion, 1 medium

Celery, 3 stalks

Parsley

Low-fat or fat-free
mayonnaise

Sugar-free applesauce

Lemon, 1

Golden Delicious apples,
3 large

Assorted root vegetables,
1 ½ pounds

Menu #5

Spicy Sesame Noodles

Marinated Red Onions

Stir-Fried Zucchini and Mushrooms

Two popular tastes come together in this quick-to-fix Thai-inspired dish. Use
rice vinegar, if available; otherwise, mix equal parts of plain white vinegar and
water. You'll find chili oil and toasted sesame seeds in Asian markets and some
regular supermarkets.

Spicy Sesame Noodles

——— 6 ———

makes 4 large servings

1/4 cup creamy peanut butter

3 tablespoons water

3 tablespoons rice vinegar, or 1 1/2 tablespoons each white vinegar and water

2 tablespoons tamari or soy sauce

1 tablespoon finely minced fresh ginger

2 to 3 teaspoons Oriental chili oil, or to taste

1 teaspoon sugar

1 teaspoon dark sesame oil

8 ounces whole wheat angel hair pasta or soba noodles

3 tablespoons toasted sesame seeds

2 scallions (green parts only), thinly sliced on the diagonal

1. In a blender or food processor fitted with a steel blade, combine peanut butter, water, vinegar, tamari or soy sauce, ginger, chili oil, sugar, and sesame oil. Blend or process until very smooth.

2. Cook pasta in boiling water according to package directions, or until al dente; drain well and combine with sauce. Scatter sesame seeds and scallions over all; serve at once.

Helpful Hint: If using soba noodles, cook 5 minutes, drain well, and combine with sauce.

Marinated Red Onions

— ❀ —

makes 4 servings

1 tablespoon canola oil

¼ teaspoon salt

¼ cup rice vinegar, or 2
tablespoons each white
vinegar and water

2 medium red onions, peeled and
thinly sliced

1. Combine oil, salt, and vinegar in a cup or small bowl. Drizzle marinade over
onions, toss lightly with a fork, and set aside 10 minutes, or until slightly wilted.

Stir-Fried Zucchini and Mushrooms

— ❀ —

makes 4 servings

1 tablespoon canola oil

½ pound sliced fresh mushrooms

3 medium unpeeled zucchini, cut
in ½-inch dice

1 large clove garlic, minced

2 tablespoons tamari or light soy
sauce

1. Heat oil in a large skillet over medium-high heat. Add mushrooms and cook
quickly, stirring, until they begin to brown slightly, 2 to 3 minutes. If mushrooms
start to release liquid, raise heat to high and cook until it evaporates.

2. Add zucchini and garlic; stir-fry another 3 to 4 minutes. Add tamari or soy
sauce; toss to combine, and serve.

Shopping List for Menu #5

Pantry Staples

Oriental chili oil

Dark sesame oil

Toasted sesame seeds

Peanut butter

Rice or white vinegar

Tamari or soy sauce

Canola oil

Sugar

Whole wheat angel hair pasta or soba noodles

Garlic, 1 large clove

Salt

Refrigerator/Freezer Staples and Perishables

Red onions, 2 medium

Fresh ginger root

Scallions, 2

Mushrooms, 1/2 pound

Zucchini, 3 medium

Red onions, 2 medium to large

Menu #6

Tofu Scallops with Red Pepper Sauce

Wilted Spinach with Sesame Seeds

Cucumber and Dill Salad

Hot Rolls with Garlic Butter

Tofu has made its way from the esoteric to the mainstream because it is convenient, easy to use, and a source of high-quality protein. Bland, the way pasta is, tofu is convenient for all kinds of sauces, toppings, and flavor-enhancers.

Tofu Scallops with Red Pepper Sauce

6

makes 6 servings

2 pounds extra-firm water-packed
tofu

3 tablespoons olive oil, divided

1 medium Bermuda or Spanish
onion, peeled and coarsely
chopped

1 large clove garlic, peeled and
sliced

2 tablespoons fresh lemon juice

2 large red bell peppers, roasted or
jarred

Salt and freshly ground black
pepper to taste

Ground paprika

Tabasco or other hot pepper sauce

½ cup green olives stuffed with
pimiento, sliced

2 tablespoons finely minced
cilantro or parsley

1. To press tofu: Drain tofu and wrap in a kitchen towel. Place in colander. Place a
heavy can on top. Set aside 15 to 20 minutes.

2. In a large skillet, heat 1 tablespoon oil over medium-high heat; add onion and
cook, stirring, 1 or 2 minutes. Add garlic, cook, stirring, 1 more minute, and add
lemon juice. Bring to a boil, then transfer to a blender or food processor fitted
with a steel blade.

3. Add peppers; process mixture to a purée, scraping down sides of container as
needed. Return purée to skillet; season with salt, pepper, paprika, and Tabasco
or other hot pepper sauce to taste. Stir in olives and let sauce heat gently 2 to 3
minutes over low heat.

4. Cut each piece of tofu into scallop-sized cubes; season on both sides with salt
and pepper. In a clean skillet, heat remaining 2 tablespoons oil over medium-
high heat; add tofu and cook, stirring, on all sides until lightly golden. Transfer
to paper towels to remove excess oil.

5. To serve, divide tofu between dinner plates. Spoon hot red pepper purée over
and scatter with cilantro or parsley.

Wilted Spinach with Sesame Seeds

—————— 6 ——————

makes 4 servings

1 pound fresh spinach, stemmed, or two 10-ounce packages frozen whole-leaf spinach

2 teaspoons dark sesame oil

Salt and freshly ground black pepper

1/4 cup toasted sesame seeds

1. Wash spinach leaves. Lift spinach from water, but do not dry. (They will cook in the water that clings to the leaves.) If using frozen spinach, thaw in a microwave oven or overnight in refrigerator; drain well in a strainer.

2. Heat a large skillet. Add sesame oil and spinach. Stir-fry over high heat 1 or 2 minutes, until thoroughly heated through and wilted. Sprinkle with salt and pepper to taste. Scatter toasted sesame seeds over and serve.

Cucumber and Dill Salad

———— 6 ————

makes 4 servings

1 large English (seedless) cucumber, washed and peeled (if waxed)

Salt

3 tablespoons white vinegar

3 tablespoons cold water

3 tablespoons sugar or brown rice syrup

2 tablespoons minced fresh dill or 1 teaspoon dried dill weed (not seed)

1. Slice cucumber thinly; lay in a colander in the sink. Sprinkle lightly with salt to taste and let drain 10 minutes.

2. In a small bowl, combine vinegar, water, and sugar or brown rice syrup; mix well to blend. Add cucumber and dill; mix well. Serve at once or chill, covered, until needed.

Shopping List for Menu #6

Pantry Staples

Extra-virgin olive oil

Dark sesame oil

Toasted sesame seeds

Paprika

Tabasco or other hot pepper sauce

White vinegar

Sugar or brown rice syrup

Salt

Fresh black pepper

Garlic, 1 large clove

Refrigerator/Freezer Staples and Perishables

Bermuda or Spanish onion, 1 medium

Lemon

Green olives stuffed with pimiento, 1/2 cup

Fresh cilantro or parsley

Fresh dill or 1 teaspoon dried dill weed (not seed)

Extra-firm water-packed tofu, 2 pounds

Red bell peppers, 2 large

English cucumber, 1 large

Fresh spinach, 1 pound, or frozen whole leaf spinach, two 10-ounce packages

Whole grain dinner rolls

Menu #7

Spaghetti Squash with Julienne of Vegetables

Stuffed Tomato Salad

Hot Garlic Bread

Achieve a truly sterling effect by combining spaghetti squash with aromatic vegetables, enhancing it further with fresh herbs. There are several ways to cook a large squash like this: bake, microwave, or boil. The easiest is boiling.

Spaghetti Squash with Julienne of Vegetables

— 6 —

makes 4 servings

1 large (4-pound) spaghetti squash

2 teaspoons canola oil

½ teaspoon dark sesame oil

2 medium cloves garlic, minced

2 medium carrots, finely julienned or grated

1 red bell pepper, cut into long slender strands

¼ cup water

¼ cup tamari or soy sauce

Salt and freshly ground black pepper to taste

2 zucchini, dark part only, cut into long slender strands

5 to 6 fresh basil leaves, chopped, or 1 teaspoon dried basil

¼ teaspoon crushed red pepper

¼ cup grated Parmesan cheese

½ cup chopped toasted pecans (see note)

1. Place whole squash in a large pot with enough water to cover. Bring to a boil, lower heat, and simmer 30 minutes, or until you can easily pierce skin with a fork. Remove from water; cool. Cut squash in half lengthwise; remove and discard seeds. Pull the strands out of shell with a fork into a large bowl.

2. Heat oils in large skillet or wok. Add garlic; cook, stirring, briefly, then add carrots, bell pepper, water, tamari or soy sauce, and salt and pepper. Stir, then gradually add spaghetti squash. Stir-fry over high heat 4 to 5 minutes, until carrots are crisp-tender.

3. Add zucchini, basil, red pepper, and half of the Parmesan. Continue to stir-fry over high heat another 3 minutes. Spoon mixture onto a large serving platter, top with remaining Parmesan, and scatter with pecans. Serve at once.

Note: To toast pecans, preheat oven to 325°F. Place pecans in a single layer on a shallow baking sheet. Toast until brown.

Stuffed Tomato Salad

— 6 —

makes 4 servings

3/4 cup vegetable stock or water

2/3 cup quick-cooking brown rice

2 teaspoons canola oil

1 small onion, minced

4 medium ripe tomatoes

Salt and freshly ground black
   pepper to taste

1 tablespoon fresh lemon juice

1/2 cup chopped walnuts or pecans

1/2 cup chopped parsley

4 tablespoons grated Parmesan
   cheese

1. In a small saucepan, bring stock or water to a boil. Add rice; cover and simmer on low heat 10 minutes. Transfer to a mixing bowl; cool.

2. In a small skillet, heat oil. Add onion and cook, stirring frequently, until onion is translucent and limp. Add to rice in mixing bowl.

3. Cut tops off tomatoes; scoop out and discard cores and seeds with a small knife. Turn tomato cups upside down to drain a few minutes, then turn right side up and sprinkle to taste with salt and pepper.

4. Add lemon juice, chopped nuts, parsley, and salt and pepper to rice-onion mixture. Divide evenly among tomato shells and sprinkle each with 1 tablespoon Parmesan.

Shopping List for Menu #7

Pantry Staples

Canola oil

Dark sesame oil

Pecans

Walnuts

Salt

Fresh black pepper

Vegetable stock

Quick-cooking brown rice

Tamari or soy sauce

Crushed red pepper

Garlic, 2 medium cloves

Refrigerator/Freezer Staples and Perishables

Grated Parmesan cheese

Onion, 1 small

Carrots, 2 medium

Spaghetti squash, 1 large

Red bell pepper, 1

Zucchini, 2

Fresh basil leaves, 1 small bunch, or dried basil

Lemon, 1

Parsley

Tomatoes, 4 medium

Garlic bread, 1 loaf

Menu #8

Vegetable Curry with Lentils

Basmati Rice

Cucumber and Radish Raita

Pita Pocket Bread or Flatbread

Lentils are a powerhouse of nutrients, including protein, complex carbohydrates, and soluble fiber, which has been proven to reduce cholesterol levels. They come in various shades of green, brown, and the vivid orange indigenous to East Indian cuisine. Cook them 20 minutes if using for salads, and twice as long for soups and stews.

Vegetable Curry with Lentils

—— 6 ——

makes 4 servings

1 tablespoon canola oil

2 medium onions, cut into wedges

1 medium carrot, peeled and sliced on the diagonal

1 stalk celery, sliced on the diagonal

3 medium cloves garlic, chopped

2 teaspoons curry powder, or to taste

1 teaspoon ground cumin

1/8 teaspoon dried red pepper flakes, or more to taste

2 to 2 1/2 cups vegetable stock

1 cup brown or green lentils

3 small Redskin or 2 medium Yukon Gold potatoes, cubed

One-half 10-ounce package frozen cut green beans, or 1 cup fresh beans

One-half 10-ounce package frozen green peas, or 1 cup fresh peas

1 cup plain low-fat yogurt

2 tablespoons minced cilantro or parsley for garnish

1. In a large skillet, heat oil over medium heat. Add onions, carrot, and celery. Cook 10 minutes, stirring frequently. Add garlic; cook 2 minutes more. Add curry powder, cumin, dried red pepper flakes, stock, lentils, and potatoes. Raise heat; bring stew to a simmer.

2. Cover and simmer over low heat 15 minutes, or until lentils are nearly tender. Add green beans; cover and cook 5 minutes more. Add green peas; cover and cook 5 minutes more. Remove pan from heat, uncover, and allow the stew to cool slightly before stirring in yogurt. Garnish with minced cilantro or parsley.

6 ——————— 6
To keep parsley, cilantro, and asparagus fresh longer, stand upright, stems down, in a jar of water, like flowers in a vase. Cover loosely with a plastic bag and refrigerate. Change the water every other day.
6 ——————— 6

Basmati Rice

———— 6 ————

makes 4 servings

2 cups water

1 teaspoon salt

1 cup brown Basmati rice

1. In a medium saucepan, bring water and salt to a rolling boil. Add rice; reduce heat to a simmer, cover tightly, and cook 20 to 25 minutes or until all liquid is absorbed. Remove cover and fluff with a fork.

Cucumber and Radish Raita

———— 6 ————

makes 4 servings

2 cups plain low-fat yogurt

1 medium cucumber, peeled, seeded, and finely chopped

3 red radishes, trimmed and finely chopped

½ teaspoon ground cumin

½ teaspoon salt, or to taste

Freshly ground black pepper to taste

Cayenne pepper (optional)

Chopped cilantro or parsley

1. In a bowl, combine yogurt, cucumber, radishes, cumin, salt, and pepper.

2. To serve, sprinkle with additional black pepper (if desired), cumin, cayenne pepper, and chopped cilantro or parsley.

Shopping List for Menu #8

Pantry Staples

Brown or green lentils

Brown basmati rice

Canola oil

Curry powder

Ground cumin

Dried red pepper flakes

Cayenne pepper (optional)

Vegetable stock

Redskin (3 small) or Yukon Gold (2 medium) potatoes

Garlic, 3 medium cloves

Salt

Fresh black pepper

Refrigerator/Freezer Staples and Perishables

Plain low-fat yogurt, 3 cups

10-ounce package frozen cut green beans (unless using fresh)

10-ounce package frozen green peas (unless using fresh)

Onions, 2 medium

Carrot, 1 medium

Celery, 1 stalk

Cilantro or parsley

Cucumber, 1 medium

Red radishes, 3

Pita bread

Menu #9

Mache Chowder

Pan Bagna

Fresh Fruit

Iced Tea

It might look and even taste Italian, but Pan Bagna is Cajun, hailing from Louisiana. In cities like New Orleans, these tangy marinated salads/sandwiches are sold for quick lunches and afternoon snacks. Precede its spiciness with a creamy corn soup based on Mache, another famous Louisiana dish.

Mache Chowder

—————— 6 ——————

makes 4 servings

2 teaspoons olive oil

¼ large green bell pepper, finely minced

1 medium stalk celery, finely minced

1 small onion, finely minced

1 clove garlic, minced

One 15-ounce can cream-style corn

3 ¾ cups skim milk, soymilk, or rice milk

1 tablespoon yellow miso paste

Salt and white pepper to taste

3 tablespoons finely minced parsley

1. In a medium saucepan, heat oil over medium heat. Add green pepper, celery, onion, and garlic. Cook, stirring constantly, until vegetables wilt and are tender but not brown.

2. Add corn and milk to mixture; stir to blend. Cook, stirring constantly, until warm. Add miso paste, salt, and white pepper. Cover and simmer over very low heat about 5 minutes, or until heated through. Stir in parsley and serve at once.

Pan Bagna

—————— 6 ——————

makes 4 servings

If your bread isn't completely fresh, try steaming it. Wrap bread slices, pita, etc., in a small towel and place in a steamer or on a rack set over gently boiling water. In 1 to 2 minutes, you'll have a pliable, tantalizing bread. If you prefer to use a microwave, place bread inside a slightly moist paper bag in the microwave set on medium power for 20 to 30 seconds.

6 ounces feta cheese

1 medium green bell pepper, halved, cored, and thinly sliced

1 medium red bell pepper, halved, cored, and thinly sliced

4 tomatoes, halved, cored, and coarsely chopped

1 small red onion, peeled, halved, and thinly sliced

1 medium cucumber, peeled, seeded, and coarsely chopped

3 ounces Kalamata or other Greek black olives, pitted and chopped

½ cup chopped walnuts

½ cup finely sliced parsley

1 teaspoon dried Italian herb blend

1 clove garlic, minced

3 tablespoons olive oil

3 tablespoons red wine vinegar

Salt and black pepper to taste (optional)

4 round hard rolls

Fresh basil leaves (optional)

1. Crumble feta cheese into a mixing bowl. Add green and red peppers, tomatoes, onion, cucumber, olives, walnuts, parsley, herb blend, garlic, oil, and vinegar. Toss lightly until well combined. Season to taste with salt and pepper, if desired. Set aside.

2. Cut off top third of each roll with bread knife. Pull out soft insides of each roll to form an indentation; fill with salad and replace tops, pressing down lightly with your hand. Serve remaining salad alongside each with a garnish of fresh basil leaves, if desired.

Shopping List for Menu #9

Pantry Staples

Extra-virgin olive oil

15-ounce can cream-style corn

Salt

White pepper

Walnuts

Dried Italian herb blend

Red wine vinegar

Fresh black pepper (optional)

Garlic, 2 cloves

Refrigerator/Freezer Staples and Perishables

Skim milk, soymilk, or rice milk

Yellow miso paste (available in refrigerator case at natural food stores)

Onion, 1 small

Red onion, 1 small

Celery, 1 stalk

Parsley

Green bell pepper, 2 medium

Red bell pepper, 1 medium

Feta cheese, 6 ounces

Tomatoes, 4 medium

Cucumber, 1 medium

Kalamata or other Greek black olives, 3 ounces

Round hard bakery rolls, 4 large

Fresh basil, 1 small bunch (optional)

Menu #10

Spiced Tomato Juice

Submarine Special

Old-Fashioned Potato Salad

Now and then, it's nice to make room for a big submarine sandwich. The one in this menu has it all: contrasting textures and tastes, all of it piled high onto a garlicky bean-spread base. Add avocados, crunchy sprouts, lettuce, tomato, and a garnish of toasted sunflower seeds to make this recipe unforgettable.

Spiced Tomato Juice

———— 6 ————

makes 4 servings

One 48-ounce can V-8 or tomato
  juice

1 tablespoon vegetarian
  Worcestershire sauce, or more to
  taste

2 tablespoons fresh lemon juice

Tabasco sauce to taste

Freshly ground black pepper to
  taste

2 medium stalks celery, cut into
  strips for stirrers

1 small lemon, thinly sliced, for
  garnish (optional)

1. Combine all ingredients except celery and lemon in a refrigerator container; chill thoroughly. Serve in glasses with sticks of celery for stirring and garnish with lemon, if desired.

Submarine Special

—————— 6 ——————

makes 4 sandwiches

Two 15 ½-ounce cans cannelini beans, drained and rinsed

½ cup sliced fresh parsley

¼ cup fresh lemon juice

¼ cup olive oil

2 large cloves garlic, finely minced

1 tablespoon fresh (1 teaspoon dried) tarragon

Freshly ground pepper to taste

Salt (optional)

4 whole grain submarine or hoagie rolls

2 avocados, halved, pitted, and thinly sliced

Pickled cherry or jalapeño peppers (optional)

2 medium tomatoes, thinly sliced

1 small head Boston or Bibb lettuce, finely shredded

1 small box fresh alfalfa or other sprouts

3 tablespoons dry-roasted sunflower seeds

Low-fat or nonfat Italian dressing

1. In a food processor fitted with a steel blade, process beans, parsley, lemon juice, olive oil, garlic, tarragon, and pepper until smooth. Add salt if desired.

2. Slice submarine or hoagie rolls in half; pull out soft insides of each roll to form an indentation and spread approximately ¹/₂ to ³/₄ cup of bean spread on each bottom half. Top bean spread with avocado slices, hot peppers, tomatoes, lettuce, sprouts, and a sprinkle of sunflower seeds.

3. Drizzle Italian dressing to taste over all; cover with top roll halves. Serve at once.

Old-Fashioned Potato Salad

— 6 —

makes 4 servings

2 ½ pounds unpeeled Redskin or
Yukon Gold potatoes

Pinch salt (optional)

1 small red onion, finely diced

1 large stalk celery, finely diced

2 tablespoons sweet pickle relish

½ cup finely chopped parsley

Salt and freshly ground black
pepper to taste

3/4 cup reduced-fat mayonnaise

1. Place potatoes into a large heavy saucepan. Cover with cold water and salt; bring to a full boil. Cover, reduce heat to medium-low and cook 20 to 30 minutes, or until potatoes can be pierced easily with a fork. Drain potatoes and set aside until they can be handled comfortably. (Don't allow to cool completely.) Cut into ½-inch cubes.

2. In a large mixing bowl, combine potatoes, onion, celery, pickle relish, and parsley. Salt and pepper to taste. Add mayonnaise in ¼ cup increments, tossing, until salad is lightly coated with dressing. Chill or serve at room temperature.

Instead of separating parsley leaves from stems before chopping them, do as professional chefs do: Tie the bunch together and thinly slice what you need from the top, tender stems and all. Put the remainder back in its "vase," cover, and refrigerate. Continue slicing from the bunch as needed until only coarse stems and a few leaves are left.

Shopping List for Menu #11

Pantry Staples

Extra-virgin olive oil

Dry-roasted sunflower seeds

Vegetarian Worcestershire sauce

Tabasco sauce

Fresh black pepper

Salt

Two 15 ½-ounce cans cannellini beans

Garlic, 2 large cloves

Redskin or Yukon Gold potatoes, 2 ½ pounds

Refrigerator/Freezer Staples and Perishables

Pickled cherry or jalapeño peppers (optional)

Low-fat or nonfat Italian dressing

Reduced-fat mayonnaise

Sweet pickle relish

Fresh or dried tarragon

Parsley, 1 bunch

Red onion, 1 small

Celery, 3 stalks

Lemon

Whole grain submarine or hoagie rolls, 4

Avocados, 2

Tomatoes, 2 medium

Boston or Bibb lettuce, 1 small head

Alfalfa or other sprouts, 1 small box

48-ounce can V-8 or tomato juice

Menu #11

Black Bean Enchiladas

Orange, Radish, and Onion Salsa

Spicy Mexican Rice

Black Bean Enchiladas

makes 4 servings

2 teaspoons canola oil

1 medium onion, peeled and chopped

2 large cloves garlic, minced

Two 15-ounce cans black beans, drained and rinsed

1 medium tomato or 2 plum tomatoes, diced

4-ounce can chopped mild, medium, or hot green chilies, undrained

1 tablespoon chili powder, or to taste

1 teaspoon ground cumin

2 tablespoons tamari or soy sauce

Salt and freshly ground black pepper

12 corn tortillas (7-inch diameter)

1 cup bottled enchilada sauce

4 ounces low-fat sharp cheddar cheese

1 pint plain low-fat dairy or soy yogurt, or sour cream

4-ounce can pitted sliced black olives

3 whole scallions, thinly sliced (optional)

1. Preheat oven to 375° F. Lightly spray a 9-by-13-inch baking pan; set aside.

2. Heat oil in a large nonstick skillet over medium heat. Add onion and garlic; cook, stirring until translucent and soft, about 5 minutes. Add beans, tomato, canned chilies with juices, chili powder, cumin, and tamari or soy sauce. Bring to a boil, stirring frequently. Lower heat, cover, and simmer 10 minutes. Uncover and continue simmering about 5 minutes, or until liquid reduces and mixture is firm and holds its shape. Season to taste with salt and pepper.

3. Fill a medium bowl with warm water and dip tortillas to soften. Place a tortilla in baking dish, spoon 2 heaping tablespoons of filling down the center, and roll. Push filled tortilla to the far end of dish. Continue dipping tortillas in water, draining, filling, and rolling, placing the filled enchiladas in a single layer.

4. Spoon sauce over rolls and scatter with cheddar cheese. Cover dish with foil and bake 20 minutes, or until bubbly hot. Serve with garnishes of yogurt or sour cream, black olives, and scallions.

Orange, Radish, and Onion Salsa

6

makes 4 servings

1 large Navel or Temple seedless orange, peeled, cored, and chopped

1 1/2 cups chopped red radishes

1 medium red onion, peeled and roughly chopped

1 or 2 jalapeño peppers, seeded, cored, and finely minced

3 tablespoons olive oil

1 tablespoon red wine vinegar

1 tablespoon minced cilantro or parsley

Salt and freshly ground pepper to taste

1. Place chopped orange in a medium mixing bowl or serving dish. Add radishes, onion, and jalapeño peppers.

2. In a cup, combine oil, vinegar, cilantro, and salt and pepper. Whisk with a fork, drizzle over salad, and toss to combine.

Peppers aren't fiery just to the tongue. Capsaicin, the chemical that makes peppers "hot," can also burn your skin and eyes. When handling and preparing hot peppers, it is wise to wear plastic or rubber gloves, because the capsaicin can remain on your hands for hours, even after washing.

If your palate becomes ablaze with too much heat, the best remedy is to drink or eat a dairy product, such as milk, ice cream, or yogurt. Dairy products have a protein called casein, which washes away the capsaicin. Eating starchy food or drinking water or alcohol doesn't have much effect and sometimes intensifies the heat.

Spicy Mexican Rice

—————— 6 ——————

makes 4 servings

1 ³/₄ cups water

2 ¹/₂ cups quick-cooking brown rice

Pinch salt and freshly ground black pepper

Pinch cayenne pepper

2 teaspoons ground cumin

2 teaspoons canola oil

¹/₃ cup hulled green pumpkin seeds

2 tablespoons minced cilantro or parsley

1. In a medium saucepan over high heat, bring water to a boil. Add rice; cover, reduce heat, and cook 10 minutes. Remove from heat and uncover. Add salt, pepper, cayenne pepper, and cumin. Set aside.

2. Heat oil in small heavy skillet over medium heat. Add pumpkin seeds and cook 3 minutes or until lightly toasted, shaking pan frequently. Transfer seeds to a paper towel to drain. Fluff rice with a fork; stir in pumpkin seeds and cilantro or parsley.

Shopping List for Menu #11

Pantry Staples

Two 15-ounce cans black beans

4-ounce can chopped mild, medium, or hot green chilies

Quick-cooking brown rice

Canola oil

Chili powder

Ground cumin

Tamari or soy sauce

Extra-virgin olive oil

Red wine vinegar

Cayenne pepper

Fresh black pepper

Salt

Garlic, 2 cloves

4-ounce can pitted sliced black olives

Refrigerator/Freezer Staples and Perishables

Cilantro or parsley

Red onion, 1 medium

Onion, 1 medium

Tomato, 1 medium or 2 plum tomatoes

Corn tortillas, package of 12 (7-inch diameter)

Enchilada sauce, 1 small bottle

Low-fat sharp cheddar cheese, 4 ounces

Low-fat dairy or soy yogurt or low-fat sour cream, 1 pint

Scallions, 1 small bunch (optional)

Navel or Temple seedless orange, 1 large

Red radishes, 1 package

Jalapeño peppers, 1 or 2

1 1/2-ounce package pumpkin seeds

Menu #12

Cassoulet

Spinach and Radicchio Salad with Mustard Vinaigrette

Oven-Heated French Bread

This savory bean casserole from the Languedoc region of France is traditionally made with duck and sausage. This vegetarian version proves that there's more than one way to adapt an old tradition. Use seitan (wheat gluten) or tempeh (soybean cakes), and you won't miss the meat one bit.

Cassoulet

—————— 6 ——————

makes 4 large servings

1 teaspoon olive oil

1 medium onion, diced

2 medium carrots, peeled and diced

2 parsnips, peeled and diced (1 large rutabaga may be substituted)

3 large cloves garlic, minced

8 ounces seitan or tempeh, cut into ½-inch cubes

2 ½ teaspoons Herbes de Provence or Italian herb blend

½ teaspoon dried basil

½ teaspoon dried rosemary

1 tablespoon Dijon mustard

½ teaspoon salt

Freshly ground black pepper, to taste

2 cans Navy or Northern white beans, drained and rinsed

2 cups vegetable stock

1 loaf French bread

2 tablespoons minced parsley

2 tablespoons minced scallions

1. Preheat oven to 350° F. In a heavy casserole dish, cook the onion, carrots, parsnips, and garlic in oil, stirring, over medium-high heat until tender and lightly browned, about 15 minutes.

2. Add seitan or tempeh, Herbes de Provence or herb blend, basil, rosemary, mustard, salt, pepper, beans, and vegetable stock to cover. Cover and bake 45 minutes to 1 hour.

3. After baking, stir and adjust seasonings to taste. Warm French bread in oven 10 minutes before end of baking time. Before serving, add minced parsley and scallions; stir lightly.

Spinach and Radicchio Salad with Mustard Vinaigrette

6

makes 4 servings

1 large bunch fresh spinach, stems removed, cut into bite-size pieces

1 small head radicchio, cut into bite-size pieces

Vinaigrette:

3 large whole scallions, finely minced

1 tablespoon Dijon mustard

3 tablespoons olive oil

3 tablespoons red wine vinegar

1/3 cup apple juice

1. Combine spinach and radicchio in a salad bowl; set aside. In a small mixing bowl, combine scallions, mustard, oil, vinegar, and apple juice. Whisk with a fork until frothy and emulsified. Pour over salad, toss, and serve at once.

Shopping List for Menu #12

Pantry Staples

Extra-virgin olive oil

Red wine vinegar

Herbes de Provence or
Italian herb blend

Dried basil

Dried rosemary

Canned vegetable stock

Garlic, 3 large cloves

Fresh black pepper

Salt

2 cans Navy or Northern
white beans

Refrigerator/Freezer Staples and Perishables

Apple juice

Dijon mustard

Onion, 1 medium

Carrots, 2 medium

Parsley

Scallions, 1 bunch

Parsnips, 2 medium

Seitan or tempeh, 8 ounces

Fresh spinach, 1 large bunch

Radicchio, 1 small head

French bread, 1 loaf

Menu #13

Moroccan Vegetable Tagine with Couscous

Cucumbers with Garlic Yogurt

Pita Bread

Moroccan Vegetable Tagine with Couscous

——————— 6 ———————

makes 4 servings

2 teaspoons margarine

1 medium Spanish or Bermuda sweet onion, cut into thin wedges

2 cups vegetable stock

1 teaspoon ground cumin

1 medium carrot, cut into matchsticks

1 large red bell pepper, cored, seeded, and cut into strips

1 large yellow bell pepper, cored, seeded, and cut into strips

15-ounce can chickpeas, drained and rinsed

Salt and freshly ground pepper to taste

1 medium zucchini, trimmed, quartered, and cut into 1-inch pieces

8 ounces precooked couscous

3 tablespoons minced cilantro or parsley

1. Heat margarine in a heavy medium saucepan. Add onion and cook, stirring, until soft but not brown, 2 to 3 minutes. Add vegetable stock, cumin, carrot, red and yellow bell peppers, and chickpeas. Season with salt and pepper. Bring mixture to a boil, then reduce heat to low, cover, and cook 2 minutes.

2. Stir in zucchini and couscous, cover tightly, and remove from heat. Set aside 5 minutes to steam. Uncover and toss lightly to distribute vegetables. Before serving, add cilantro or parsley and toss again.

Cucumbers with Garlic Yogurt

—————— 6 ——————

makes 4 servings

2 large cucumbers, seeded and
thinly sliced

1 small red onion, thinly sliced

¼ cup rice vinegar, or white
vinegar and water in equal
amounts

1 tablespoon fresh lemon juice

1 large clove garlic, minced

1 tablespoon minced basil, parsley,
or thyme, or a mixture

Salt and freshly ground pepper to
taste

¾ cup plain low-fat dairy yogurt
or soy yogurt

1. Slice cucumbers and onion. Place in a medium mixing bowl; set aside. In a small
bowl, mix vinegar, lemon juice, garlic, herbs, and salt and pepper to taste. Stir
in yogurt; pour over cucumbers and onion. Cover, chill, and toss before serving.

Shopping List for Menu #13

Pantry Staples

Rice or white vinegar

Ground cumin

Canned vegetable stock

Salt

Fresh black pepper

15-ounce can chickpeas

Garlic, 1 large clove

Refrigerator/Freezer Staples and Perishables

Margarine

Plain low-fat dairy yogurt or soy yogurt

Red onion, 1 small

Carrot, 1 medium

Cilantro or parsley

Lemon, 1 large

Red bell pepper, 1 large

Yellow bell pepper, 1 large

Spanish or Bermuda onion, 1 medium

Zucchini, 1 medium

Precooked couscous, 8 ounces

Cucumbers, 2 large

Basil, parsley and/or thyme

Pita bread

Menu #14

Cincinnati Chili

Braised Baby Carrots

Zucchini-Jícama Salad

Cornbread

In Cincinnati, you can have chili just about any way you want it. Two-way brings it ladled over a steaming bowl of hot spaghetti noodles. Three-way, they top the two-way version with shredded cheese; four-way adds some chopped onion, and five-way means red kidney beans have been added to the spaghetti. Confused? Why not try Coney style, a vegetarian hot dog on a bun topped with mustard, chili, onions, and cheese? First, the chili has to have a tad of chocolate to give it its characteristic taste.

Cincinnati Chili

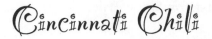

makes 6 to 8 servings

16-ounce can red beans

16-ounce can chickpeas

2 medium onions, coarsely
chopped

4 cloves garlic, minced

1 medium carrot, peeled and
chopped

1 large stalk celery (including
leaves), chopped

4 cups water

6-ounce can tomato paste mixed
with 1 cup water

½ teaspoon ground allspice

1 teaspoon ground cumin

1 ½ teaspoons ground cinnamon

3 tablespoons chili powder, or to
taste

½ ounce unsweetened baking
chocolate

2 tablespoons red wine vinegar

1 bay leaf

1 tablespoon vegetarian
Worcestershire sauce

Salt and freshly ground black
pepper to taste

1. Combine all ingredients in a heavy large soup kettle or stew pot. Bring to a full
rolling boil, stirring occasionally to prevent sticking.

2. Reduce to a simmer and cook, uncovered, until thick enough to mound on a
spoon, about 1 hour. Adjust salt and pepper to taste.

> **Dried herbs and spices lose
> their flavor and potency after
> about a year. It's best to buy
> them in the smallest possible
> amounts and store them in tightly
> closed bottles in a cool, dry
> spot out of direct light.**

Braised Baby Carrots

6

makes 4 servings

1 pound baby carrots, peeled

Salt

2 tablespoons margarine, divided

1 ½ teaspoons sugar

1. In a medium skillet, place carrots and sprinkle with salt. Add 1 tablespoon margarine and enough cold water to come halfway up sides. Bring to a boil, reduce heat to low, cover, and cook 5 to 8 minutes or until a fork can pierce carrots. Uncover, raise heat, and rapidly boil away most of the remaining liquid.

2. Add remaining margarine and sugar; cook, stirring constantly, 1 to 2 minutes, or until carrots are glazed.

Zucchini-Jicama Salad

6

makes 4 servings

1 medium jicama, peeled and grated on large-hole grater

1 medium zucchini, unpeeled and grated on large-hole grater

1 small red onion, chopped

3 tablespoons minced cilantro or parsley

½ cup fat-free red wine vinaigrette dressing

1. Place jicama and zucchini shreds into a serving bowl. Scatter onion over top, then follow with cilantro or parsley. To preserve bright colors, add dressing right before serving.

Shopping List for Menu #14

Pantry Staples

Ground cinnamon

Chili powder

Ground allspice

Ground cumin

Bay leaf

Unsweetened baking
chocolate

Red wine vinegar

Vegetarian Worcestershire
sauce

Sugar

Salt

Fresh black pepper

Garlic, 4 cloves

16-ounce can red beans

16-ounce can chickpeas

6-ounce can tomato paste
mixed with 1 cup water

Refrigerator/Freezer Staples and Perishables

Fat-free red wine vinaigrette
dressing

Margarine

Onions, 2 medium

Red onion, 1 small

Carrot, 1 medium

Celery, 1 stalk

Cilantro or parsley

Baby carrots

Jícama, 1 medium

Zucchini, 1 medium

Cornbread

Further Reading

Vegetarian Times Complete Cookbook, by the Editors of *Vegetarian Times* with Lucy Moll (Macmillan, 1995).

The Vegetarian Epicure and *The Vegetarian Epicure, Book Two,* by Anna Thomas (Vintage Books, 1972, and Alfred A. Knopf, 1978).

The Moosewood Cookbook, by Mollie Katzen (Ten Speed Press, 1992).

The New Laurel's Kitchen, by Laurel Robertson, Carol Flinders, and Brian Ruppenthal (Ten Speed Press, 1986).

Ten Talents, by Rosalie and Frank Hurd (Self-published, 1983).

The American Vegetarian Cookbook, by Marilyn Diamond (Warner Books, 1990).

The High Road to Health: A Vegetarian Cookbook, by Lindsay Wagner and Ariane Spade (Prentice Hall, 1990).

Tofu Cookery, by Louise Hagler (The Book Publishing Company, 1991).

Vegetarian Pleasures: A Menus Cookbook, by Jean Lemlin (Knopf Publishers, 1987).

Amazing Grains: Creating Vegetarian Main Dishes with Whole Grains, by Joanne Saltzman (H.J. Kramer Inc., 1990).

CHAPTER 4

It's Time for Some Real Health-Care Reform

BY NOW, YOU FEEL LIKE YOU'RE REALLY GETTING THE HANG OF THINGS. YOU CAN DISCUSS BASIC VEGETARIAN NUTRITIONAL CONCEPTS WITH EVEN THE BIGGEST DOUBTER. AND YOUR FAMILY? YOU COOKED UP A MEATLESS MEAL OR TWO FOR THEM, AND MIRACLE OF MIRACLES, THEY DIDN'T REVOLT. THIS VEGETARIAN STUFF IS A LOT EASIER THAN YOU HAD EVER EXPECTED, SO YOU'VE SETTLED DOWN ON THE COUCH TO TAKE IN THE NEXT CHAPTER. GOOD JOB, VEGGIE BEGINNER. WE'D LIKE TO REWARD YOU WITH TWO SIMPLE WORDS: GET UP. YES, GET UP. SET DOWN YOUR BOOK, GO TO THE NEAREST MIRROR, AND TAKE A LOOK AT YOURSELF. THEN COME BACK AND WE'LL TALK.

Now that you've returned, ask yourself a couple of simple questions:

Do I feel good, both physically and mentally?

Am I doing everything I can for the body that looked back at me in the mirror so it can thrive, rather than simply survive?

You've learned that a vegetarian diet is nutritionally sound. And you've found that the food is hardly boring, brown, or bland. But don't forget why you picked up this book in the first place: You were hoping that a vegetarian lifestyle could benefit you in various ways, and now we're ready to start discussing those payoffs. Here is where we start to talk about the whys of vegetarianism, as we've already answered the whats and hows. Here is where we start to show you why vegetarianism can help improve that person, both inside and outside, that you just took stock of in the mirror.

In this chapter, we'll focus on the advantages of vegetarianism that affect your physical well-being. How does what you eat influence the likelihood that you will develop (or avoid) diseases like cancer, heart disease, or diabetes? And if you are already at a point where you have damaged your body through a long period of unhealthful living, is there anything that vegetarianism can do to reverse the damage?

Don't Just Talk the Talk

BEING A VEGETARIAN DOESN'T guarantee good health; it has a great potential to do so, provided one eats the right foods, exercises, and avoids such nasty habits as smoking and drinking heavily. Trust us: There is such a thing as an unhealthful meatless diet. A diet that is dominated by dairy products, diet soda, and frozen cheese pizza is certainly vegetarian, but it doesn't do much to reduce the risk of obesity or disease. Anyone who is making a move toward going totally meatless should monitor his or her diet by keeping a diet log and taking special notice as to whether he or she is replacing high-fat, processed meat foods with high-fat, processed vegetarian foods. If vegetarianism is being approached in the correct way, whole grains, fresh vegetables, and a minority of sinful products should dominate that diet log. Getting the benefits we're about to discuss means actually taking steps to improve oneself. Talking about it doesn't make too much happen.

Evidence of this is as close as our television. Reports on the nightly news about health and how to improve it are just about as common as weather reports. Researchers tell people to avoid foods that are high in fat and cholesterol, and then the public turns around and boasts that it is following this good advice. Unfortunately, the very next report discusses how Americans are getting fatter and more unhealthy as a population. You'd think that if everyone were actually telling the truth, the results would be just the opposite.

It seems the only thing the health craze has taught Americans is what the right answers should be when someone asks them what they ate for dinner last night. Don't believe that? Consider a 1993 Food Marketing Institute survey that reported nine out of ten supermarket shoppers said they had altered their eating habits to be more healthful. And another survey conducted by the Calorie Control Council showed reduced-fat and fat-free products are more popular than ever; 137 million Americans say they choose them over the high-fat versions.

At the same time, however, results from a Centers for Disease Control study show that the number of Americans who are seriously overweight, after holding steady for twenty years at about 25 percent of the population, jumped to 33 percent in the 1980s. Another article in the *Journal of the American Medical Association* reported that fifty-eight million U.S. residents weigh at least 20 percent more than their ideal body weight, which classifies them as clinically obese. These facts are beyond interesting; for many they may wind up being deadly.

Heading Disease Off at the (By) Pass

AN OUNCE OF PREVENTION is worth a pound of cure. Of course we're still talking food, and we're still talking about its relation to disease. In this section, we'll provide you with the basic information that supports this old adage. Then we'll let you comb journal upon journal for the rest of the mountain of evidence. The following can never be said enough. While other aspects of your lifestyle do factor in (smoking, for instance), *diet is one of the most important factors affecting your risk of heart disease, cancer, and a host of other illnesses*. Improving your diet will save you time, money, and, potentially, your life. According to Walter Willett, chair of the department of nutrition at Harvard University's School of Public Health, half of all illnesses could be eliminated or greatly delayed through changes in diet. A meat-based diet provides less nutritive value than a plant-based diet at a cost (both financial and physical) that is much greater than we should have to bear. The following is a brief rundown of some of the most common diseases that affect Americans, and how a vegetarian diet is one of the best solutions for those who hope to avoid—or even for those already afflicted with—these diseases.

Heart Disease

We may as well address the No. 1 killer in America right away. Heart disease, clinically called atherosclerosis, is a degenerative condition of the arteries that progresses over time; the earliest signs of the disease can appear as early as the first year of life. It is characterized by arterial growths called plaque. When enough of the plaque accumulates, it can cause a blood clot to form. The clots have the  potential to seal off one of the arteries leading to the heart, resulting in a heart attack. Plaque also forms in the brain, causing strokes, and in the legs, causing poor circulation and pain.

A diet that is high in cholesterol and saturated fat is one of the most common causes of plaque buildup, as the main components of plaque are, you guessed it, saturated fat and cholesterol. According to Michael Murray and Joseph Pizzorno, authors of *The Encyclopedia of Natural Medicine* (Prima Publishing, 1991), men and women who have cholesterol levels of 256 milligrams per deciliter (mg/dl) or above have a five times greater risk of developing heart disease than those whose levels are below 220 mg/dl.

Also factoring in the formation of plaque are serum lipoproteins, also known as fat-carrying proteins. There are two types of serum lipoproteins: low-density lipoproteins (LDLs), which transport cholesterol to the body's tissues, and high-density lipoproteins (HDLs), which transport cholesterol to the liver for metabolism and excretion. You may have heard of HDLs referred to as "good cholesterol" and LDLs as "bad cholesterol." The ratio of HDLs to LDLs in our system plays a significant role in whether the cholesterol we are taking in is being excreted or deposited in tissues. For the record, obesity, diabetes, and smoking have all been linked to lower HDL levels.

> Another positive for vegetarians is the presence of what are known as omega-6 and omega-3 fatty acids, better known to some of us as "essential fatty acids." Researchers have found them to be effective in lowering cholesterol; these essential fatty acids are contained in vegetable oils, not animal fats.

For heart disease that is life-threatening, doctors commonly use one of two procedures—angioplasty or bypass surgery—to remedy the situation. Neither operation is cheap; *Business Week* magazine listed the cost in 1993 of a bypass operation at $43,000. In the United States, the costs of these two procedures per year add up to $44 billion. Yes, we said *billion*, and this is only for *two procedures*. The human toll is even more shocking. According to the Dallas-based American Heart Association, 42.5 percent of nationwide deaths in 1992 were the result of heart disease. In that same year as many as 1.5 million Americans had heart attacks, roughly one-third of them fatal. What's really a shame about these outrageous human and financial tolls is that they could be reduced substantially if more people made an effort to eat better, exercise, and quit smoking. For those already stricken with heart disease, 50 percent of bypass operations have to be repeated within five years if they don't change their lifestyles, and nearly half of all angioplastied arteries have clogged up again after only four to six months.

There are several reasons why switching to a vegetarian diet is one of these very effective lifestyle changes in an effort to delay or prevent heart disease. According to Murray and Pizzorno, the presence of foods high in fiber and carbohydrates (the cornerstones of a vegetarian diet) is the key to keeping heart disease at bay. In addition, the protein found in vegetables has been shown to reduce cholesterol levels, while the protein in animal products has been shown to raise these levels.

By now, vegetarianism probably isn't sounding too bad, seeing that it has the ability to have prolonged the lives of at least 50 percent of the more than 480,000 who died of coronary heart disease in 1992. And no one would complain if we were to cut $22 billion off the amount we spend on angioplasties and bypasses each year. In contrast to our $43,000 figure, twenty nutrition counseling sessions to design a meatless dietary plan run about $800, roughly 1.8 percent of what the bypass costs. According to Neal Barnard, M.D., a Washington, D.C., physician who promotes health through a vegetarian diet, only 5 percent of us actually have a hereditary tendency toward heart disease. For the rest of heart patients, the only disease factor that is hereditary in their families is a poor diet.

Even a diet containing *less* meat (which most heart specialists recommend) only slows, not stops, the buildup of plaque. So why, you ask, do many physicians recommend diets for their heart patients that will eventually kill them? And why does our government—through the use of the U.S. Department of Agriculture's Food Pyramid—recommend a diet that has been shown to promote heart disease, rather than fending it off? There are several reasons. Bad eating habits, and the heart disease that is so prevalent because of them, are so common in our society that many doctors and government officials accept them as normal. And we live in an age where drugs and surgery are regarded as the best quick fixes for a bad situation, rather than trying to prevent that situation in the first place. At this point, medical schools don't teach *prevention;* they teach *cure.*

For those who already have heart disease, there is still hope, other than through the use of drugs or surgery. This optimism comes from work by Dean Ornish, M.D., who in 1990 began publishing a string of research studies that showed that when his patients went on a very low-fat (10 percent or less calories from fat), low-cholesterol vegetarian diet, not only did a vast majority of their plaques stop growing, they actually started to shrink. Chest pain decreased. And heart patients who entered the program without much hope for recovery were actually getting up, moving around, and becoming productive once again. These were miraculous results, considering the conventional wisdom in the cardiology community that once heart disease had formed, it could only be slowed, not stopped, much less reversed.

We would be remiss unless we stressed that these improvements didn't come with a half-hearted attempt, and they didn't happen overnight. Ornish's patients made a commitment to change their diet for good, not just a couple of days per week. They stopped smoking. They lowered their cholesterol, learned how to reduce the stress in their lives (primarily through meditation), and they exercised regularly. They worked closely with Ornish to design a special diet and received genuine support from their family and friends to see them through. Their new lifestyle improved their quality of life and definitely kept them around for longer than they seemed destined to be. Everyone has the ability to take these same steps, but the first step is a real lasting commitment. After all, the $44 billion club hardly needs another member.

High Blood Pressure

Hypertension, or high blood pressure, is one of the most common reasons Americans find themselves at their doctor's office each year. According to the American Heart Association, some fifty million Americans ages six and older were affected by it during 1992. We mention it right after heart disease because its presence is associated with an increase in heart disease and death. It also increases the risk of stroke, kidney failure, and congestive heart failure. According to Murray and Pizzorno, although more than 90 percent of high blood pressure cases cannot be narrowed to one specific cause, there is considerable research that indicates a poor diet is a primary contributor to the condition.

When plaque starts to form and block the arteries, blood is forced to work harder to push through the smaller openings. This difficulty is evidenced in a rise in blood pressure readings by your physician. Typical treatments are usually in the form of drugs, which will relieve the symptoms but have a host of potentially life-threatening side effects. A better plan of action may be to forgo the drugs and control high blood pressure with changes in diet and lifestyle.

High blood pressure almost always goes hand in hand with high cholesterol. Eat a low-fat vegetarian diet, reduce your cholesterol intake, and reduce your risk of high blood pressure; it really can be that simple. Other factors affecting hypertension are stress, obesity, high salt intake, smoking, heavy drinking, and a sedentary lifestyle. Meat eaters have the highest incidences of hypertension because of the large amounts of fat and cholesterol in their diets. Ovo-lacto vegetarians have significantly less hypertension than meat eaters. Vegans are even better off.

Other than controlling cholesterol, avoiding high-sodium processed foods and keeping high-fat eggs and dairy to a minimum are all necessary to avoid high blood pressure. According to Murray and Pizzorno, a typical vegetarian diet contains fewer processed foods and more foods that are richer in the vitamins, minerals, and other substances that have been shown to help reduce high blood pressure, especially potassium, which reduces the blood-vessel-constricting effect of adrenaline during times of stress. Add a steady exercise program to all of this, and you are on the right road to getting your blood flowing—unimpeded.

Cancer

We're soon going to start sounding like a broken record, but poor diet is once again the biggest cause of cancer. According to a 1985 National Cancer Institute study, poor diet is responsible for 35 percent to 60 percent of cancer cases; smoking for about 30 percent. If you add these figures together, you'll find that 65 percent to 90 percent of all cancer cases can be avoided by breaking a couple of bad habits. And yes, studies of vegetarians show that death rates from cancer are appreciably lower than those experienced by the general population. In addition, studies of societies that consume high-fat, meat-based diets consistently have the highest rates of every type of cancer. It comes as no surprise that when cultures that have relied on a plant-based diet throughout their history (such as in Greece and Japan) start adding more meat to their menus, their rates of various cancers start to grow.

Cancers that are most directly caused by diet are sometimes known as "hormonal cancers," because eating certain types of foods increase the number of cancer-causing hormones in our bodies. Breast, prostate, and colon cancer are particularly linked to red-meat consumption.

Breast cancer is an ever-present threat for women; one in nine will be stricken with the disease. A high-fat diet has been linked to an overproduction of various estrogens (female sex hormones), which subsequently increase cancer risk. And since fats help to transport some carcinogens into the bloodstream, people who take in a high amount of fat are also enabling easier transport of toxins through their bodies. Women who take steps when they are young to improve their diet will have a better chance of avoiding the devastating effects of breast cancer.

Prostate cancer is the most common type of cancer in men, generally striking those men age forty and older. As men age, their likelihood of prostate cancer increases. High-fat, red-meat diets increase the amounts of testosterone (male sex hormones) and estrogen in men. As we have already learned, an increase in the level of sex hormones helps to promote the growth of cancerous cells. A marked increase in these hormone levels can lead to higher production of cancer cells in the prostate, eventually overcoming the body's ability to fight them.

Men and women with fat-rich diets also commonly face colon (large intestinal) cancer. The digestive juice known as bile is made in the liver and stored in the gallbladder. This bile ends up in the intestine, where it breaks down fats for absorption into the bloodstream. However, bacteria in the intestine turn the bile acids into cancer-promoting substances called secondary bile acids. The more fat we take in, the more bile acids need to be produced, thus increasing the amount of secondary bile acids produced, in turn helping to fuel the cancer. Decreasing the amount of fat that the body has to process helps to lower the amount of cancer-causing agents that enter our system.

It's important to note that most everyone has cancerous cells in his or her body at one time or another; the difference between those who get cancer and those who don't is not completely understood. But vegetarians are winning the battle against cancer not only because they are taking in less of the foods that are known to promote the growth of cancer cells but also because they are taking in more of the foods that research is showing to be cancer-inhibiting. For example, vegetarian diets are traditionally high in fiber and beta carotene, two substances that researchers believe have cancer-fighting properties. Another theory stems from research studies of the immune systems of vegetarians, which show that their white blood cell count is markedly higher than that of nonvegetarians; white blood cells battle disease. Scientists are not sure whether one of these specific factors prevents cancer, but for now, the best we can assume is that the combination of factors works together in sort of a team effort.

Diabetes

There are two types of diabetes. The first type develops when we are children, condemning us to a lifetime of taking insulin on a daily basis. Type I (juvenile) diabetes affects individuals who have a shortage of insulin due to damage to the insulin-producing cells in the pancreas. Daily injections and a watchful eye on one's diet help compensate for the body's inadequacy.

According to the American Diabetes Association, more than twelve million of the thirteen million diabetes cases in this nation occur during adulthood and are known as Type II diabetes. This form of the disease develops when the body does not produce insulin at the correct time or cannot process it correctly. The bad news is that if untreated, this disruption in the blood can cause severe eye damage, impaired kidney function, poor circulation, coma, and death. And since most Type II patients are overweight, they are also at a greater risk of heart attack and stroke. The good news is if you take care of your weight and blood sugar levels through proper diet and regular exercise, you may not need drug treatment at all.

Researchers have found that converting to a low-fat, complex-carbohydrate vegetarian diet helps the body regain its ability to process insulin. Helping matters further is the fact that foods such as whole grains, fruits, and potatoes are fiber-rich. Fiber helps slow the release of sugar into the blood, so blood sugar levels remain more even. Drinking enough water—eight glasses a day—is also important, as it helps the body to absorb nutrients and fiber.

Beginning an exercise program is the second key treatment. For most people, reducing their caloric intake may help them lose a few pounds. But if they are still leading a sedentary lifestyle, any weight reduction from that point on becomes very difficult. And as many of us know, when we're not eating much and not losing any weight, things can get quite frustrating, and we wind up forgetting about the whole diet altogether. Getting ourselves into shape helps break the ten-pound barrier and keep the weight off. Whether you choose to walk, play tennis, swim, or jog really doesn't matter. Doctors recommend that the combination of proper diet and exercise is the best way to reduce blood sugar and help the body's insulin convert glucose into energy.

Osteoporosis

From the time we are children into early adulthood, our bones are growing and becoming stronger as they prepare to anchor our adult figure. But as time marches on, the process can reverse, and bone mass is lost, a condition called osteoporosis. This disease is most common in postmenopausal women (who tend to lose the most bone mass), and can result in fractures from accidents or falls. In its advanced stages, tiny fractures of the vertebrae may cause the spine to bend, producing the hunched-back posture we see in some elderly women.

There is currently a debate raging in the medical community about what exactly causes osteoporosis. Some say it comes from not getting enough calcium when we are young. But there is a growing number of researchers and physicians who believe that the amount of calcium our bodies get is only crucial up to a point; what matters from that point on is our ability to retain the calcium our diet provides us. An overload of protein, which we discussed in Chapter 2 (pages 20–21), can cause the body to excrete calcium at a higher rate, a process now believed to be one of the prime contributors to the disease.

Dairy products have universally been touted as the best way to get calcium, but the amount of protein they contain may cause us to lose calcium at the same time we're gaining it. New research suggests that a diet that limits protein to recommended levels and exercise throughout a woman's life are vitally important to the prevention of osteoporosis.

Intrigue in the Islands

By now, you probably realize that if we eat too many fatty foods, smoke, drink heavily, and don't exercise, we're putting ourselves at a higher risk for obesity, cancer, and heart disease. But what happens when an entire culture that was once predominantly agriculturally based (the United States is one example of this) becomes wealthier and begins to consume a more affluent diet, namely one that is dominated by meat and other animal products? Can the damage be undone with a return to the diet of old? Terry Shintani, M.D., M.P.H., J.D., looked to the history of the Hawaiian Islands to find the answers to those questions.

When Captain Cook arrived in Hawaii in 1778, his men carried illnesses such as measles, mumps, and smallpox. Thousands of Hawaiians died when they contracted these diseases because they had no previous exposure, so they had built up no immunity. Even worse was the meat-based diet that was introduced by the flood of Americans who followed Cook during the 1800s, as it soon replaced the plant-based diet to which the Hawaiians were accustomed. As the new diet became more entrenched, diet-related diseases which were once unheard of rapidly became the leading killers of a once very healthy society. Today, native Hawaiians are twice as likely as the average American to die from heart disease, cancer, and stroke; four times more likely to die from infectious disease; and six times more likely to die from diabetes.

The ancient Hawaiian diet was based on fiber-rich, high-carbohydrate plant foods such as taro, sweet potatoes, bananas, and leafy greens; fish and chicken were eaten only occasionally. Shintani, who runs Hawaii's largest public health clinic, hypothesized that if he were to reintroduce his patients to the lower-fat, plant-based diet that once dominated the Hawaiian culture, he could improve their failing health. And he was right. When they changed their diet, Shintani's patients' overall health improved, while reliance on medications was reduced or eliminated. Shintani can't say for sure which foods helped fight which diseases specifically, which brings up the question: Do vegetarian diets promote health because of an absence of animal products, or do plant-based foods have some sort of healing ability? As we saw in the various sections on the specific diseases, the answer is probably a combination. One thing is crystal clear, though: Animal-based diets, because of their life-threatening fat and cholesterol, have not made good on their claims of being able to function as the anchor for a healthful human diet.

Hit the Road, Jack

So THERE YOU ARE with a bowl of vegetarian chili in hand, your book in the other as you head for the couch. You eat a healthful lunch while reading through the section on diet's role in the prevention of disease, and a smile slowly crosses your face. You recline on the couch, remote control in hand, knowing you've kept your fat intake down, you're not smoking—you've got heart disease, cancer, and diabetes beat, right? There's just one other thing you need to do. You're on the right track so far, but now, literally speaking, you need to hit the track.

This is usually where everyone lets out a groan simultaneously, but if you really want to achieve optimal health, you've got to get a move on, at least a couple of times per week. There is little argument in the scientific community regarding exercise's complementary role to diet in the prevention of numerous

diseases and chronic conditions. Simple walking on a regular basis can help prevent osteoporosis in some women, and some form of cardiovascular exercise helps to strengthen the heart muscle and many of your other muscles for the long haul ahead. Keeping active in the here and now helps ensure that you will be able to remain active when you are older.

How do diet and exercise work together to promote health? If you are exercising, but eating a high-fat diet, plaque can still develop in your arteries, and you are still at risk for numerous types of cancers. Conversely, if you take the step to cut your fat, you're still taking in a couple thousand calories per day. If your daily exercise consists of walking from the car into the office in the morning, you're not burning off too many of those calories. You may lose a few pounds, but you won't want to keep yourself on such a restrictive diet, and you may find yourself slipping. Eventually, you'll probably gain all

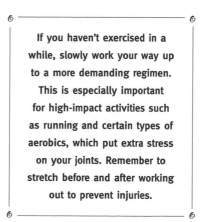

If you haven't exercised in a while, slowly work your way up to a more demanding regimen. This is especially important for high-impact activities such as running and certain types of aerobics, which put extra stress on your joints. Remember to stretch before and after working out to prevent injuries.

that weight back, losing your grip on better health. What's more, as we age, our metabolism slows, meaning that your body will be using even fewer of those calories if you don't do anything to work them off.

We know that not all of us are cut out for the health club scene and not all of us are gifted athletes. This matters very little, as there are many more physical activities in life than hitting the basketball court. For those who want to include exercise in their lifestyle but don't want to train for a triathlon, walking is a sensible alternative. A thirty-minute walk every day or a one-hour walk three or four times per week will cover about eight miles and, more important, improve muscle tone and burn up about 1,000 calories. Add a low-fat vegetarian diet to that, and you've got a start at a formidable plan to be healthy. Take a look at what some of these activities can do to help you get rid of some of the calories you're taking in:

> Strength-building exercises not only burn calories; they increase muscle mass. Increasing your muscle-to-fat ratio will increase your metabolism, even when you're not exercising.

APPROXIMATE CALORIES BURNED PER THIRTY MINUTES OF ACTIVITY

Activity	185-pound man	125-pound woman
Basketball (vigorous/full-court)	538	364
Bicycling (13 mph)	394	266
Cross-country skiing (8 mph)	577	390
Golf (twosome)	250	169
Jogging (5 mph)	333	225
Rowing (vigorous)	538	364
Running (8 mph)	577	390
Swimming (55 yd/min)	488	330
Tennis (beginner)	178	120
Walking (4.5 mph)	266	180

SOURCE: *JOHNS HOPKINS COMPLETE GUIDE FOR PREVENTING AND REVERSING HEART DISEASE*, BY PETER O. KWITEROVICH, JR., M.D. (JOHNS HOPKINS UNIVERSITY PRESS, 1993).

The only way you'll stick with an exercise program is to find something that you like doing. If you like to jog every morning, by all means do it. But if you'd like something more low impact, you don't have to look very far to find it. Do you like to dance? Do you like to play tag with your children or take your dog on long walks around the neighborhood? Once you get into an enjoyable routine of exercise, it will be something that you look forward to on a daily basis. And weight loss won't be the only indication that your body is undergoing a change. You'll look better, you'll feel better, and you'll probably be able to handle the stresses of your day better. Exercise is not only healthful for the body, but it is also therapeutic for the mind.

Healing the Natural Way

AS YOU KNOW BY NOW, many vegetarians view their eating habits as just one piece of an entire lifestyle puzzle. There are vegetarians who were first interested in animal welfare and the environment; they turned to vegetarianism out of compassion. Then there are others who turned to vegetarianism for health reasons, only to realize after a year or two the environmental benefits of a vegetarian diet. Being a vegetarian falls along a continuum of natural, compassionate living, with natural medicine being another point along the continuum.

Of course this doesn't mean that all vegetarians take part in natural medicine, just as all people who practice natural medicine aren't vegetarians. It just seems that for many, vegetarianism and alternative medicine fit together in a special way. You may find you want to use natural methods not only to help prevent disease, but also to help yourself heal when you are sick. Here is a brief reference to just a few different types of alternative medical practices that you many want to examine more closely. If you're already undergoing conventional treatments, ask your doctor how these supplemental healing methods can fit in to your overall health plan.

CHIROPRACTIC. This is an alternative therapy that has become so common in our society that many think it's now rather conventional. The goal of chiropractic treatment is to open up the vertebrae to release tension and pressure on the nerves, restoring normal nerve function. This is accomplished by manipulating the spine. Some patients benefit from treatment on the first visit, but a greater number may require treatments over a period of a few weeks or even months to show appreciable improvement.

Although chiropractors are not permitted by law to prescribe drugs or perform surgery, they must complete a lengthy course of study similar to that of a traditional medical doctor. Students must complete two years of undergraduate study at a recognized college or university, followed by a four-year course at an accredited chiropractic college that includes all courses studied by M.D.'s with the exception of pharmacology.

ACUPUNCTURE. This is an ancient Chinese treatment based on a theory that the body must be in balance to function properly. It employs the Taoist theory of *qi*, or life force, which flows through the body along specific pathways known as *meridians*. If any factor—such as poor diet or stress—is blocking the flow of the life force, illness results. To right the energy flow, acupuncturists insert very fine needles into points along the meridians. Acupuncturists sometimes supplement the needle treatment with moxibustion (burning Chinese herbs at key points of the body) and cupping (placing of glass cups over certain areas to regulate blood flow).

The length of treatment varies from case to case, depending on how local and severe a particular condition is. Since most acupuncture patients seek treatment only after exploring many conventional options, it is important for the acupuncturist to take a thorough history of the patient in order to see what has been attempted to remedy the condition. Acupuncture is not licensed in every state, although to be accredited, practitioners must take a three-year course of study.

HOMEOPATHY. This method of natural healing originated in Germany and was brought to the United States in the nineteenth century. It is based on the principle that like cures like. Homeopaths treat their patients with remedies made up of substances which in larger doses would produce the same symptoms as the illness. You only have to look as far as conventional medicine to understand what we mean. When we are vaccinated, we are usually given small doses of the pathogen that causes the disease, so our bodies can fight the battle on their own and gain immunity as only a natural process can achieve. Homeopaths work in the same way. The principle is to give the smallest dose possible to stimulate the body's own defenses against the disease.

AYURVEDA. This is a system of healing that came to us from India, and is based on the principle that different personality types get sick in different ways; to treat the illness, you must adapt the treatment to the individual. Ayurveda generally employs such therapies as massage, meditation, and lifestyle adjustments in different combinations to strengthen the immune system.

To determine treatment, an ayurvedic practitioner must first decide which of the three distinct body categories, or *doshas*, you fit into. To do this, he or she will ask specific questions about your health and lifestyle. After learning your dosha, the ayurvedic practitioner will develop a treatment program and may suggest methods of diet, exercise, and stress reduction to put your body back into balance. There is no national certification program for ayurveda, but there are several training programs that range in length from one to three years.

Miracle Cure, or Mirage?

LIGHT BULBS. AUTOMOBILES. AIRPLANES. ANTIBIOTICS. What do they all have in common? Most of us are taught to believe that they are among the greatest inventions of our time. In the case of antibiotics, we have been taking them with abandon for years to ward off bacterial infections of all types, with great

success. But with many great inventions, there is a catch. Bacteria are smarter than we thought. Over time, they have learned to find a way to outsmart antibiotics, and some diseases are getting more difficult to contain. Researchers are constantly trying to update antibiotics to combat sicknesses that were once easily controlled. The reason for this emerging phenomenon is our abuse and overuse of antibiotics over the past fifty years or so.

One of the greatest abuses of antibiotics occurs on farms. Farmers regularly feed more than fifty antibiotics to their herds—more than twenty-five million pounds per year—in an effort to stave off disease that runs rampant through their dirty and overcrowded pens. As more antibiotics are used, disease becomes more resistant, making even more antibiotics necessary. When the animals are killed and eaten, there are still traces of these antibiotics in their flesh. Many researchers now believe that consistently ingesting antibiotics may cause disease to become slower to leave. In the cases of food-borne bacteria such as salmonella, outbreaks of human sickness have been traced to sick animals that weren't cured by antibiotics, because the strains had become too strong and resistant.

Vegetarians can't even count themselves among the safe ones, as bacteria travel easily from animals to people via their hands, dust, flies, or rodents. A mere gust of wind can transport antibiotic-resistant bacteria to people who don't even live within several miles of a farm. Milk and milk products also carry traces of antibiotics, something that ovo-lacto and lacto-vegetarians need to be aware of.

Overuse (and misuse) of antibiotics by many of us to cure illness is another problem. For bacterial illnesses, the drugs have often proven to be a miracle cure, but this has caused a high demand and overprescription of them for viral diseases such as flus and colds, illnesses that antibiotics are not able to battle. And those who take their prescription for two or three days and then quit when they start to feel better are putting their system even more at risk. The first few pills will kill off the weak bacteria, but if the medicine's full course is not followed, hardier strains can survive and flourish, resulting in prolonged and more potent illness. If the leftover bottle is used for a future condition without a prescription, further problems can occur, as there is only half of a drug that was not prescribed for that particular illness anyway. If you are taking an antibiotic, take the entire course of the medicine and don't share a prescription with anyone else. It was prescribed for you and you alone to take in its entirety.

Food-Borne Illnesses

As MORE AND MORE food passes through processing plants and less thorough inspection occurs, it is increasingly falling on the consumer to avoid the many known pathogens that commonly occur in food. Going vegetarian solves much of your problem, because one of the prime sources for contamination is meat. But if you eat eggs, for instance, you need to be extremely vigilant about what you eat and how you prepare it. Because ovo-lacto vegetarians are still in danger of some types of food poisoning, and this is the level of vegetarianism you will most likely be striving for in your early stages, we'll provide you with a guide to some of the most common types of food poisoning.

Typical food-poisoning symptoms are unpleasant but short-lived. They include nausea, vomiting, diarrhea. and abdominal cramps. Headaches, fever, and muscle weakness may also occur. Levels of illness depend on the level of contamination, so be sure to see your health practitioner if you think you may have food poisoning.

BOTULISM. One of the most serious forms of bacteria shows up most frequently in canned goods. It is actually fairly rare, but to safeguard against it, date canned or bottled foods as soon as you bring them home and discard those that are more than a year old or are in swelling or bulging cans or in glass containers with bulging lids. Other signs of botulism in canned goods include discolored contents, spurting when the can is opened, and a clouding of normally clear liquids.

SALMONELLA. Salmonella is the most common cause of food poisoning and is found mainly in meat, poultry, and eggs. Avoid foods prepared with raw or undercooked eggs. These may include homemade mayonnaise, Caesar salad dressings, mousses, meringues, homemade eggnog, true hollandaise sauce, uncooked custard pie fillings, sunnyside up or over-easy eggs, or any eggs that are soft or runny. Symptoms begin twelve to twenty-four hours after eating contaminated food.

STAPHYLOCOCCAL POISONING. This is a bacteria that occurs naturally in skin and nasal passages and is passed on via unclean hands, coughing, and sneezing. Toxin-producing staph germs multiply rapidly, especially in cream or egg sauces, custards, or starchy salads, such as potato. Symptoms begin from one to eight hours after food is eaten, and include nausea, diarrhea, and vomiting. After providing you with a few of the more memorable hours of your life, staphylococcus will generally be subdued by your body's defenses and disappear within one to three days.

CLOSTRIDIUM. This bacteria taints meat and other high-protein foods that are undercooked or left standing too long without refrigeration (on steam tables, for example, in cafeterias and all-you-can-eat restaurants). Symptoms begin six to twenty-four hours after tainted food is eaten.

Athletes with the Veg Edge

IF AFTER ALL THIS time you're still unconvinced that a combination of healthful diet and exercise is a winning combination, why not look to people who are always trying to maximize their body's potential—professional athletes? From runners to tennis players to bodybuilders, more and more athletes are forgoing meat and finding that their performances have improved as a result. The days of using a high-protein diet to build both muscle and endurance are quickly disappearing. Indeed, many athletes are beginning to find out that this diet can actually decrease bodily output, rather than enhance it.

Bodybuilders have long been viewed as hulking men who need their meat for the protein it takes to build big muscles. So when bodybuilder Andreas Cahling decided to become a vegetarian in 1979, many of his friends questioned his move. But after successfully competing as a professional for thirteen seasons, including being named bodybuilding's Mr. International, the now middle-aged Cahling has proved even the biggest doubters wrong. He encourages others to follow in his footsteps not only because of his success but also because of scientific evidence that indicates the normal high-protein bodybuilding diet can cause more harm than good. One problem with a high-protein diet is the buildup of uric acid, which can lead to urinary tract stones, gout, and arthritis in the joints, a problem for some bodybuilders. And as we have mentioned

Choosing to Live, and Live Well

THROUGHOUT THIS CHAPTER, we've examined how powerful food really can be. It can supply you with the nutrition you need and make you feel energetic and alive. It can also make you fat and sluggish and in many cases contribute to illness or even death. With your knowledge of this, there can be no better choice

---

numerous times, a high-protein diet has been linked to the leaching of calcium from the body, which can eventually weaken bones. None of these symptoms is desirable for someone trying to project the perfect body. Vegetarian athletes are asking why, when you are training your heart out to participate in an athletic event, you would take foods into your body that put a high amount of stress on your system and may force you to quit doing the thing you love much sooner than you wanted to? Remember, this attitude is from the people who are looking for the perfect body, not the rest of us who are just trying to maintain basic health. If it's good enough for them, it sure is good enough for the average American.

Other vegetarian athletes have achieved the highest honors in their individual sports. Recently retired tennis star Martina Navratilova credits a whole-foods vegetarian diet for her ability to stay at the top of her game into her late thirties. When asked if she gets enough protein, she replies, "Look at me. Do I look like I need more protein?" The list goes on from Cahling and Navratilova. Home-run champion Hank Aaron. Tennis champion Billie Jean King. Marathon winner Gary Fanelli. Olympic bronze medalist in wrestling Chris Campbell. Their combination of healthful eating and healthful living has helped them to achieve, and will continue to help them achieve for years to come, no matter what they find themselves doing.

you make than to reform your diet as soon as you can. You might think that heart disease, strokes, and osteoporosis always happen to someone else or to someone older than you. But if you're currently eating a high-fat, meat-based diet, you may be allowing these diseases to gain a foothold in your body. Blockages don't just appear overnight; they build up over time. Our bones don't become brittle one morning when we wake up; they deteriorate over the years. Everyone needs to start now to be able to avoid disease later, and from what we've seen from the research, it's never too late.

Maintain a reasonable weight for your age, sex, height, and frame. Reduce the amount of fat you eat to no more than 20 percent of your total calories. Find other ways to season your food besides salt and butter. Go outside and get some exercise, at least a few days per week. The common theme here is moderation. We're not asking you to shun every food you have always loved but rather to be smart about food, and understand how it affects your body. The gift of a healthful life is the most ample reward you'll ever receive, and you have the power to make sure you do a good job at it.

Recommended Reading

Dr. Dean Ornish's Program for Reversing Heart Disease, by Dean Ornish, M.D. (Random House, 1990).

The Encyclopedia of Natural Medicine, by Michael Murray, N.D., and Joseph Pizzorno, N.D. (Prima Publishing, 1991).

Food for Life: How the New Four Food Groups Can Save Your Life, by Neal Barnard, M.D. (Harmony Books, 1993).

The Natural Pharmacy, by Miriam Polunin and Christopher Robbins (Collier Books, 1992).

Perfect Health and Quantum Healing, by Deepak Chopra, M.D. (Harmony Books, 1991).

Compassionate, Clean, and Green

*A*S CHILDREN, WE'RE TAUGHT TO TRY TO FIND A SILVER LINING IN EVERY DARK

CLOUD, TO MAKE LEMONADE WHEN LIFE GIVES US LEMONS. BUT LATELY, IT SEEMS LIKE IT'S

GETTING MORE DIFFICULT TO FIND A BRIGHT SIDE WHEN DISCUSSING OUR ENVIRONMENT.

EVERYWHERE YOU LOOK, THERE IS ANOTHER NEWS REPORT ON HOW OUR RAIN FORESTS

ARE DISAPPEARING AT ALARMING RATES, HOW THE GREENHOUSE EFFECT IS ALREADY

AFFECTING US, AND HOW MILLIONS OF ANIMALS CONTINUE TO SUFFER FOR THE SAKE OF

FOOD AND FURS, DESPITE THE CONSISTENT EFFORT OF CONSERVATION GROUPS. IT GIVES

MANY A FEELING OF HELPLESSNESS; BECAUSE THE SCOPE OF THESE PROBLEMS IS GLOBAL,

THE RAMIFICATIONS OF THEIR POTENTIAL OUTCOMES ARE SO SWEEPING.

Don't despair. Though it seems as if you can't do much to alleviate problems halfway across the world or even halfway across your hometown, individuals have tremendous power to help decide the fate of our land, water, and wildlife. Simply by eliminating meat from your diet, you'll be doing your share to save the environment, and you'll be saving the lives of countless numbers of animals who would have suffered inhumane treatment on their way to your plate.

In this chapter, we'll show you why vegetarianism is so beneficial to both flora and fauna and why, if more people went vegetarian, we would be on our way to turning back the clock to a day when the potential benefits we could get from our planet seemed limitless. To empower you even further, we provide hints and tips on how you can live your life more Earth-friendly and cruelty-free. When you're done reading, you'll see that though our global problems can be quite daunting, their solutions need to come from individuals on a local basis. All it takes is enough people who care to make a real difference.

Environmental Condition: Critical

THE SKY IS A crystal-clear blue and a gentle breeze blows through the treetops. Cows softly moo in the distance, going about their own business, while pigs happily slop around in their muddy bliss. Farmer John is out in the fields, tenderly tending to the soil as his father and his grandfather before him did. His wife is in the barn, feeding the horses and chickens as another day on the farm slowly passes by.

Sounds like something you'd see on a postcard, doesn't it? The American farm: A kinder, gentler place to be. But is this really what the average American farm is like? Well, sometimes yes, but mostly no. The notions that we grew up with about how food is produced in this country have not changed, even though the people who actually produce the food discarded them years ago. Food is now a big business. America's small farm has vanished over the past thirty years. Fewer than 2 percent of owners now control more than 33 percent of U.S. farmland, according to a 1988 study by the U.S. Department of Agriculture's Economic Research Service. The goal of most of these large farms is return on investment; i.e., get as much out of the land as quickly as possible. The environmental impact is a secondary consideration, if it is a consideration at all.

Farms particularly dominated by this production-oriented mentality are those that "produce" beef, poultry, and pork. We'll talk more about the animals themselves in the next section, but first we'll view the environmental impact of producing meat versus producing grain, and it is eye-opening. You may be surprised to learn that though a pound of ground beef will run you about $1.50 at the grocery store, what that meat is really costing the Earth is priceless, precious natural resources that cannot be replaced. Here is a brief rundown of why trading beef for beans is beneficial to the environment:

Land

Take a look out over America's amber waves of grain, and you'll probably think you're looking at rows and rows of food that will end up on somebody's table. Actually, about two-thirds (64 percent) of the land you see is being used to grow grain or soybeans that will go to the cows, chickens, pigs, and other animals that will eventually end up on someone's plate. This may not seem that disheartening, but consider that roughly one-quarter of the world's total population (about 1.3 billion people) could be fed with this grain. Think about it. If we could cut the amount of grain that is used for livestock *by only 10 percent* and use it instead for public consumption, 130 million people could be fed. In 1993, researchers from Tufts University in Medford, Mass., reported that twelve million American children go to bed hungry each night. A good start would be to feed them with this food we should be growing for humans, not hamburger.

To make matters worse, many researchers believe that the row-planting of corn, the most commonly used food for livestock feed, accelerates the erosion rate. According to the U.S. Soil Conservation Service, about four million acres of cropland are being lost to erosion in this country each year. With diminishing amounts of topsoil, it will be increasingly difficult to grow crops in subsequent years. But right now, we're essentially farming our land to death (and wasting the topsoil) so we can grow grain that will only see our tables in the form of animal products.

Can't the forces of Mother Nature keep up with this loss of topsoil? Yes, but only if we lose about five tons of topsoil per acre per year, a rate that one-third of our land is already exceeding, according to the U.S. Department of Agriculture. It stands to reason that if we are slowly killing off one-third of our land, we're going to have to find new land to replace it, or farm the heck out of the land we have to achieve increased production. If we overfarm the land, using ever-increasing amounts of pesticides and herbicides, we will wind up stripping that land of its ability to produce in subsequent years. This type of "slash-and-burn" agriculture will at best decrease the amount of food we get from an acre of soil. At worst, it could lead to food shortages for future generations.

When the animals aren't feeding at feedlots, they are overgrazing our rangelands. Each year, millions of acres of vegetation are razed by grazing animals. When all of the greenery in a particular area has been devoured, ranchers move the herd to another position. But what happens to that barren land that the voracious cattle have left behind? Without enough vegetation for protection, topsoil that is rich in nutrients and minerals is left vulnerable to wind and heavy rain. When these inevitable forces of nature act on the topsoil, it is washed away, leaving ground that is devoid of nutrients at what could have been food-growing levels.

Water

Remember those little water cycle diagrams you used to look at in grade-school science class? They showed that condensation led to clouds that led to rain that led to runoff into our streams, lakes, and rivers, beginning the cycle again? Among other things, the diagrams explained the synergy between the cycles of water and land, and showed us that what we do to our land we are indirectly doing to the water that will eventually travel over or be absorbed by that land. From this, we can safely assume that if meat production is harming our land, it's also harming our water.

Statistics from the Environmental Protection Agency (EPA) bear this out. According to the EPA, agriculture is the largest non-point source of water pollution (pollution that occurs at a point other than the point of the water source; i.e., through the ground) in this country, most of it due to livestock manure. In Frances Moore Lappé's *Diet for a Small Planet* (Ballantine Books, 1991), she reports that animal waste in the *United States alone* amounts to more than two billion tons per year, which is equal to the waste of almost half the world's human population. This livestock waste is rife with toxic chemicals, including ammonia, nitrates, herbicides, and pesticides. Untreated waste eventually leaches into the ground through decomposition and is spilled into our lakes, streams, and rivers. Continued waste runoff into these water sources can cause oxygen depletion and, in turn, an overgrowth of algae. If this cycle is allowed to continue over time, once-thriving water populations can be choked off, effectively killing the water source. And let us not forget that these toxins become part of the groundwater supply just as much as they do rivers and streams, affecting not only the water that other animals live in, but the water that people drink.

Livestock production doesn't only pollute water, it wastes a great deal of it as well. According to the U.S. Department of Agriculture, 50 percent of all water used in this country is used during some phase of livestock production. It takes 2,500 gallons of water to produce one pound of beef, but only twenty-five gallons of water to produce one pound of wheat. Not only do the animals drink the water, but the food that is used to feed them must be grown with something. And while rainfall produces a portion of this water, irrigation must be used to water areas that don't get their fair share of rain.

Much of the food that is grown for consumption by livestock is grown in the Great Plains states, an area that must get a good portion of its water from irrigation. One way that farmers irrigate their fields is through the tapping of underground aquifers, lakes that have been formed over millions of years from groundwater seepage. Frances Moore Lappé reports that scientists believe that the formation of these aquifers occurs so slowly that they should be considered non-renewable resources. Much of the Plains states' water comes from the Ogallala Aquifer, a massive underground lake that extends from western Texas to Nebraska. Though this aquifer has been a rich source of irrigation water for years, new estimates are reporting that at the rate it is being drained, it could very well be dry within the next thirty years. The main culprit? Overuse of the water for livestock purposes.

Other Natural Resources

Besides water and land, we are all well aware of the doom and gloom that has been predicted regarding the supplies of other vital fossil fuels such as coal and oil. You'll remember that in the first chapter, we provided you with a statistic that it takes seventy-eight calories' worth of fossil fuel to get one calorie of protein from beef, while it takes only two calories of fossil fuel to get one calorie of protein from plant food. Thus we are putting a lot more energy into the production of meat and meat products than we are getting out of them—by a long shot.

Then there is the amount of energy that it takes to run the equipment, run the farms and stockyards, ship animals to slaughter, and so on, and we see that we are putting a lot of energy into meat products that are not giving us much back in return. Precious resources that could be used to feed hungry members of the world's population are wasted, leaving us in doubt as to whether we will have adequate amounts of resources to last into the foreseeable future. When you examine all of the tolls, it is amazing how much the developed world's consumption of meat is putting humankind in jeopardy. It sure shows you why the potential cost of that pound of ground beef is so much greater than the $1.50 price tag on the wrapper.

A Painful Price to Pay for Animals

A TOPIC THAT NO ONE likes to think about, much less discuss, is the daily abuses that farm animals endure on the majority of factory farms that produce the majority of our nation's meat. But these abuses are an unfortunate reality, and they may be one of the reasons you are thinking twice about opening that package of chicken for dinner tonight. Our goal in this section is not to shock you, but rather to simply state the facts about what life is really like for cattle, pigs, and chickens down on the farm. If you are interested, there are many books and animal-welfare groups that you can consult for further information.

> Eating locally grown, seasonal produce not only supports the farmers in your area, but also saves the resources involved in transporting food long distances.

It is a very common human behavior to forget that steaks come from cows, bacon comes from pigs, and drumsticks come from chickens. It's not too hard to figure out why the meat industry believes that you'd be less likely to be drawn to a plastic package that is labeled "dead cow," rather than "ground beef." To the shopper, the ground beef is just that; there is little identification with the fact that what is under the wrapper was once a living, breathing animal who probably suffered on the way to the meat case. We're fairly certain that if we polled 100 average meat-eating Americans, all of them would probably say that they don't support animal abuse. Yet they continue to buy meat, showing how effective the meat industry has been in derailing one of our most common sympathies; they have taken away the faces, and they have taken away the names.

The less-than-desirable conditions of factory farms that will affect nearly every one of these animals from farm to processing plant have been well documented since the days of Upton Sinclair's *The Jungle*, but these portrayals have either fallen on deaf ears or been brushed aside by those who would rather not think the worst.

The abuse starts when an animal is born, taking the form of procedures such as branding with hot irons, removing (or docking) of the tail, teeth cutting, debeaking with hot irons, and castration. All of these procedures are administered without any anesthetic. In most cases, newborns are separated from the mother at birth; in other cases, they are forced to feed from their mothers at an accelerated pace in order to facilitate rapid growth. The idea behind both of these practices is the faster these animals reach maturity, the faster they can be converted to meat.

Life only worsens for most of the animals when they are full grown. Chickens are packed together in wire cages so small that they cannot walk by the time they are ready for slaughter. Veal calves are fed only a diet of iron-poor gruel, so their flesh will retain the certain light-colored, tender charac-

Farming for a Brighter Future

WHILE LIVESTOCK PRODUCTION is responsible for many environmental problems, improper use of land for plant foods also can be partially to blame. In both cases, harsh methods of farming strip the land rather than protecting it so it can be reused far into the twenty-first century. But now, some farmers (approximately 5,000 of the nation's 2.1 million farms) are using what are known as organic techniques. If you are looking to do more for the Earth, supporting these organic farmers is a worthwhile effort.

Food is said to be organic when it is produced without man-made chemicals; this means crops grown without synthetic fertilizers, pesticides, or herbicides. The foods are also minimally processed to maintain integrity and freshness. Organic farmers fertilize with organic waste and mineral-bearing rocks, and control pests through a variety of means that include planting early, using pest-resistant plant strains, and rotating their crops. By using the soil more naturally and efficiently, organic farmers help ensure that they will be able to continually reap the benefits from their plot of land, rather than seeing overall production decline over time. They are the nurturers of the land who seem to have all but disappeared.

When buying organic food, make sure it is "certified organic," or grown according to a code of standards that is verified by state or private organizations. Verification includes inspecting farm fields and processing

teristics that patrons of restaurants and grocery stores desire. After only a short time of confinement in darkness with little or no exercise, the cows, chickens, and pigs begin to exhibit behaviors that if demonstrated by a human would indicate severe mental illness. What's more, in order to counter the diseases that run rampant in overcrowded conditions, all the animals are fed their daily diet full of antibiotics and other drugs.

The unfortunate truth is that we are being rather tame in comparison to other publications in our description of factory-farm life. But at least you have

facilities, along with the testing of soil and water for the absence of chemicals. A National Organic Standards Board, overseen by the U.S. Department of Agriculture, was established in 1990 and as of publication time is developing guidelines that will eventually require all organic foods sold to be certified.

Organically grown produce can be less appealing cosmetically and somewhat more expensive than conventionally grown foods. This is because these foods must be harvested and marketed more quickly, and are more perishable once brought to market. Although not really more nutritious than produce grown with chemical pesticides, they are without a doubt safer for human consumption because of what they *don't* have, rather than what they do have. Products raised without synthetic chemicals are better for everyone involved, including consumers, farm workers, and the environment.

some idea about the way animals are treated on farms, and it may lead you to rethink your position on whether they should be used *en masse* for human consumption. From wherever you stand right now, you may end up in one of two common camps, believing in animal rights or in animal welfare. Most people believing in animal welfare think that humans have a right to use animals for food and clothing, but the current conditions under which these animals suffer are not acceptable. If animals are to be raised for meat, they should be raised and slaughtered in conditions that are as humane as possible. This includes providing enough space to roam, exercise, and develop normally; not forcing mothers to feed their babies twenty-four hours a day to facilitate abnormally fast growth; and keeping the animals in clean, warm, safe, spacious pens for sleeping and feeding. No matter how many people decide to continue eating meat, this program is one that is better than the current conditions.

> In a lifetime, according to the authors of *The Animal Rights Handbook* (Living Planet Press, 1990), the average meat-eating American will consume 1 calf, 3 lambs, 11 cattle, 23 hogs, 45 turkeys, 1,097 chickens, and 15,665 chicken eggs.

If, on the other hand, you believe that no one needs meat, leather, or fur and that under no circumstances should animals be harmed for human consumption, you fall more on the animal-rights side. This is the driving belief behind most U.S. animal-conservation groups, one popular example being the Washington, D.C.-based People for the Ethical Treatment of Animals. But whether *you* believe in animal rights or animal welfare is entirely based on knowing the facts and marrying them with your personal beliefs. One's stance on the rights of animals is a personal decision, one that we hope you become further educated about and make on your own.

Even if after you finish this book you decide that you don't want to completely eliminate animal products from your diet, it's still hard not to endorse animal welfare. Look at it this way: If the meat you're eating is coming from animals who for most of their lives were very frail and sick, and full of antibiotics and hormones, there is a much greater chance that sick animals will become sick meat and pass through the inspection system unnoticed. And if you are a pet owner, you certainly would feel uncomfortable if your dog or cat was forced to live in dirty, disease-ridden conditions where it got no exercise

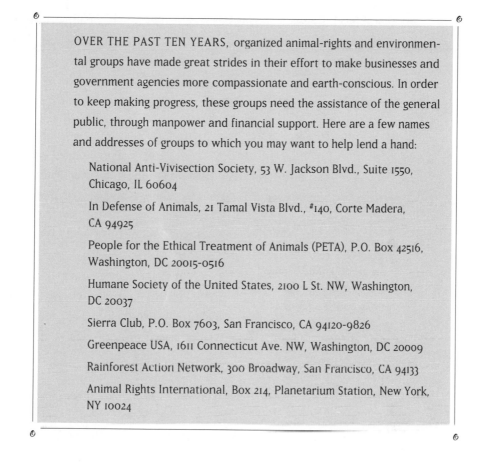

OVER THE PAST TEN YEARS, organized animal-rights and environmental groups have made great strides in their effort to make businesses and government agencies more compassionate and earth-conscious. In order to keep making progress, these groups need the assistance of the general public, through manpower and financial support. Here are a few names and addresses of groups to which you may want to help lend a hand:

National Anti-Vivisection Society, 53 W. Jackson Blvd., Suite 1550, Chicago, IL 60604

In Defense of Animals, 21 Tamal Vista Blvd., #140, Corte Madera, CA 94925

People for the Ethical Treatment of Animals (PETA), P.O. Box 42516, Washington, DC 20015-0516

Humane Society of the United States, 2100 L St. NW, Washington, DC 20037

Sierra Club, P.O. Box 7603, San Francisco, CA 94120-9826

Greenpeace USA, 1611 Connecticut Ave. NW, Washington, DC 20009

Rainforest Action Network, 300 Broadway, San Francisco, CA 94133

Animal Rights International, Box 214, Planetarium Station, New York, NY 10024

and suffered until it was killed. Cattle, pigs, and chickens all feel the same pain that dogs and cats feel; it's just that many of us look at a cow and think "hamburger," but when we look at our puppy we think "cuddly." Everywhere you look, you will find evidence that the meat industry in this country today is unhealthy, unsafe, and inhumane.

Becoming a Backyard Activist

BY NOW, IT SHOULD be fairly obvious that if individuals just like you stopped, or even substantially reduced, their meat consumption, we may have a shot at halting some of these rather ominous environmental and animal tolls which we've discussed. But over and above that, there is still quite a bit you can do on a local level to promote animal welfare and environmentalism. Here are only ten of a multitude of ways you can lead a more environmentally friendly, more cruelty-free life.

1. Choose Your Fashion with Compassion

By this, we mean avoid furs, fur-lined products, leathers, and wool products whenever possible. The methods used to trap and "harvest" minks, rabbits, raccoons, and other fur-bearing animals have long been assailed by animal-welfare groups. Newspaper articles or magazine exposés with images of injured animals suffering and dying in steel-jawed traps that have appeared over the years may pop into your mind. "Fur farms" are also extremely common, with hundreds of small animals caged for their entire lives before being killed for what in some cases only amounts to one-fortieth of a coat.

> The simple act of flushing the toilet can account for 40 percent of a home's total water usage. You can conserve up to a gallon of water every time you flush by placing two or three bricks in the tank.

And though it is easy to be sympathetic for cute bunnies, don't forget that cattle suffer for leather, and sheep suffer for wool. Most leather comes from cattle already slaughtered for their meat. You already have some idea of how they live. Similarly, many sheep who are raised for their wool live under harsh, cramped conditions.

You may be wondering just what you're going to wear to keep warm, but there are myriad synthetic alternatives on the market that are just as attractive, comfortable, and warm. You should note, however, that in some cases, these synthetic products are not environmentally friendly (i.e., they may have been made from petroleum-based products). This is indeed a downside, but at least the clothes are animal-product free. To cut down on all evils, wear your clothing until it wears out; reduced consumption is the best plan of action for *both* animals and the environment.

2. Buy Cruelty-Free Products

Twenty years ago, you could be fairly certain that the household cleaners, lipsticks, toothpastes, and shaving creams you used were tested on animals.

Now, however, animal-rights groups, through boycotts and other protests, have convinced many major companies to stop their painful eye, skin, and other tests that claimed the lives of millions of animals per year. Your best bet is to patronize companies that make products that have not been tested on animals to prove their safety and efficacy, and to make a point to not buy products that are still tested on animals.

Other methods have been designed to test products, including the use of computer programs, testing on cell cultures, or merely the use of chemical-free ingredients, which in many cases don't have to be tested. If you're interested in which companies do and don't test on animals, get your hands on a copy of *Personal Care for People Who Care*, published by The National Anti-Vivisection Society. PETA also has a guide that serves a similar purpose.

3. Recycle

Many cities and towns have mandatory recycling programs for cans, glass, and plastic, but you can easily take the recyclable mentality one step further. Develop your own personal or neighborhood recycling program to include such things as paper or newspaper. You may even want to start something through your child's school, whereby kids can get a new piece of equipment or learning materials by raising enough money through their own recycling program. Try to cut down on your initial use of these products by buying recycled paper, or using products that are biodegradable, instead of plastic packaging, when it is available.

4. Be Water-Wise

Although the level of water you use each year pales in comparison to the high level of water usage by farmers who grow their crops for livestock feed, you can still be mindful of not wasting water. Take showers, not baths. If your town has alternating-day water restrictions, observe them. And don't water your yard or garden on days when you know there is going to be rain, and don't water during the peak sunlight hours; water is best absorbed during the morning hours.

5. Don't Drive the Air Crazy

On our nation's highways, a terrifying trend is emerging. A new road is built. Cars clog it up, so another road is built. More cars clog that road up, and the cycle continues. For each new superhighway that is built, you can bet that there will be enough cars spitting out air pollution to fill it, not to mention the land that is destroyed to build all of these new roads. If at all possible, use public transportation, carpool, walk, or ride a bike, especially if the trip you're taking is only a mile or two.

6. Be a Proper Pet Owner

The world's human overpopulation problem has been well documented, but the overpopulation crisis that two of our favorite family pets are in the midst of has gone largely unnoticed. In the United States, millions of dogs and cats are born each year that cannot be cared for in loving, nurturing environments. They wind up roaming the streets or living in animal shelters. If an adoptive family is not found, the animals will eventually be destroyed. Help counter this growing problem by having your own pet spayed or neutered when it is young; and if you are in the market for a dog or cat, consider adopting from your local animal shelter.

7. Forget the Love of the Hunt

In the times long before anyone who will read this book was born, man needed to hunt to survive in harsh conditions. Today, hunting has remained popular, though any utilitarian purpose it ever served has long since disappeared. Hunters still argue that their sport is necessary to control animal populations, but since the dawn of time, the animal kingdom has done quite an adequate job of keeping itself under control. Killing for fun is no sport; in many cases, supposedly downed animals will escape and suffer over a period of days before painfully dying. To make matters worse, many hunters are not tremendously skilled and pose as great a risk to other hunters with their erratic aim as they do to the animals they are trying to kill.

8. Join an Environmental or Animal-Welfare Group

One of the best ways to learn about and participate in causes that are especially important to you is to join a group. There are numerous Earth-conscious organizations that are involved in everything from saving the whales to educating the public and legislators about the effects of acid rain on our forests. By lending a little of your time or money, you can ensure that proactive steps will continue to be taken to make our earth safer, cleaner, and more compassionate.

9. Pick Up a Broom

One of the best ways to ensure that your community stays free of litter is to organize a neighborhood cleanup crew. Join together with time and money once a month to pick up the cans, bottles, and wrappers that some folks seem to have a real problem hitting a garbage can with. Sweep up the streets. Plant some flowers in a local park. And if you live in a community that is relatively clean, think about volunteering some time in an inner-city area that is in desperate need of a neighborhood revitalization program.

> **Plant a tree. A fast-growing tree can absorb forty-eight pounds of carbon dioxide, and an acre of forest can convert 2.4 to 5 tons of carbon dioxide per year. In addition, trees prevent erosion and provide enough shade to lower air conditioning expenses in the summer.**

10. Support Nonviolence

Because of the radical acts of a few, many Americans have written off environmentalists and animal-rightists as leftist rabble-rousers. True, there have been instances of spray paintings of fur coats, destruction of animal-testing labs, and other harassment, but these in no way represent the caring, nonviolent attitude of the majority of earthwise groups. Actively voice your support for sensible, nonviolent methods of addressing animal-rights or environmental issues. Battling the insanity with insanity only serves to alienate those you are trying to convince of the worthwhile aspects of these worthwhile causes.

It All Starts with You

SAVE. REUSE. RECYCLE. CONSERVE. If this decade is to be looked upon as one that was successful in staving off some bleak environmental trends, these will have been the driving ideas behind that success. And by now, you've probably realized that you can save. You can reuse. You can recycle, and you can conserve.

When animal-rights groups began their initiative to stop manufacturers from testing their products on animals, no one believed they would get anywhere. These "radicals" certainly weren't a safe bet; they were a few people in a few groups butting heads with major corporations. But twenty years later, it is both fashionable and desirable for companies to announce they are cruelty-free. The lesson here is that if the message is good and true, it will not fall on deaf ears as long as it is continually reinforced and fought for.

Meat-eating does not conserve, reuse, or save. The lesson that statistics are telling us is that it consumes and leaves little for future generations. Vegetarianism saves food, energy, and animals, while making sure our resources will be available for years and years to come. It is without question that compassionate, clean, and green is as much a way of eating as it is a way of living everyday life.

Further Reading

Animal Liberation, by Peter Singer (Random House, 1990).

The Animal Rights Handbook—Everyday Ways to Save Animal Lives, by the Living Planet Press (Living Planet, 1990).

The Case for Animal Rights, by Tom Regan (University of California Press, 1983).

Diet for a Small Planet (20th Anniversary Edition), by Frances Moore Lappé (Ballantine Books, 1991).

Man Kind? by Cleveland Amory (Harper & Row, 1974).

Old MacDonald's Factory Farm, by C. David Coats (Continuum Publishing, 1989).

Personal Care for People Who Care (guide to cruelty-free products), by The National Anti-Vivisection Society.

Special Circumstances, Special Solutions

THROUGHOUT THIS BOOK, WE'VE USED THE TERMS "AVERAGE AMERICAN" OR "AVERAGE PERSON" WHEN COMPARING VEGETARIAN AND NONVEGETARIAN DIETS. FOR EXAMPLE, THE AVERAGE PERSON GETS "X" AMOUNT OF PROTEIN, SHOULD EAT "X" SERVINGS OF GRAINS AND VEGETABLES PER DAY, AND NEEDS TO WALK, JOG, OR SWIM "X" HOURS PER WEEK IN ORDER TO KEEP UP A CERTAIN DEGREE OF FITNESS. HE OR SHE CERTAINLY DOESN'T NEED ANY MEAT TO LEAD A HEALTHFUL EXISTENCE AND MORE THAN LIKELY COULD DO WITHOUT EGGS AND DAIRY PRODUCTS.

At times, you've probably thought that these facts and figures are all well and good, but when in our lives do we really fit into the category of average person? Doctors and nutritionists alike say that if you are a woman who is pregnant or lactating, a child, or a teenager, there are special physical characteristics that set you apart from the normal crowd. With all of these special situations, it seems as though you spend very little time being average; for much of your life you are either moving toward that point or away from it. If you happen to fall into one of these categories that aren't considered average, you may be wondering if vegetarianism is still workable for you.

There also are logistical factors that figure into a vegetarian lifestyle. It's easy enough to change your eating habits when you're the one doing the cooking, but what about when you're eating in a restaurant, at a family gathering, or at a friend's party? And then there are other considerations such as family pressures, the fact that you really *like* the taste of meat, or your geographic location that puts you miles from the nearest natural food store. We realize that there will be some bumps in your road, so like all good instruction manuals, this one will have a troubleshooting section for those times when you wonder why you considered vegetarianism in the first place.

A healthful, balanced diet that will help you avoid disease and illness in the future is a goal you should always be shooting for, no matter what your age or circumstance. We'll examine these special circumstances in this chapter, and show why vegetarianism is your best dietary route, no matter who or where you are. You average folks will probably want to read on as well, because there will probably be a time when you, or someone you are close to, aren't so average anymore.

When Baby Is on Board

EVEN WOMEN WHOSE FAMILIES have accepted their vegetarianism with little question may face a new round of doubts from their loved ones when a pregnancy is announced. And doctors who aren't well schooled in nutrition may try to convince a pregnant patient that she must eat meat to ensure proper development of the fetus. This combination of pressures for a pregnant woman, who has enough on her mind, may make her think that eating meat and saving a little hassle seem worth it. If you are the mother-to-be, here is some information to ease your mind so you can concentrate on other important things—like what you're going to name your newborn (we can't help you much there).

One of the first worries for expectant mothers is the possibility of miscarriage. Research has linked a deficiency of vitamin A in pregnant women to a higher miscarriage rate. But a 1990 study conducted by the National Academy of Sciences reported that pregnant vegetarians are more likely to get adequate amounts of vitamin A than pregnant nonvegetarians, meaning that the vegetarian women have a greater likelihood of taking their baby to term. What's more, the cornerstones of a vegetarian diet—green leafy vegetables, nuts, and whole grains—are excellent sources of folic acid, a B vitamin that is essential in the prevention of birth defects.

Another point of contention is whether a vegetarian diet can provide the proper amount of calcium, crucial to skeletal development. As you have already learned, the protein overload that is common in meat-based diets can cause calcium to be excreted before it can be absorbed, something that a pregnant woman does not need. A baby certainly doesn't need meat that commonly contains pesticide and herbicide residues from feed crops, or the traces of leftover antibiotics and growth hormones used to treat farm animals. If a vegetarian woman is taking in calcium from green, leafy vegetables or from calcium-fortified foods such as orange juice, she will most likely be better off in the calcium department than a meat-eating counterpart. Tipping the scales even more in favor of a vegetarian diet is the fact that pregnant vegetarians are more likely to take in higher amounts of fiber than nonvegetarians, which can ease the digestive problems that can be the bane of many a pregnant woman's existence.

If you are still wary about a vegetarian pregnancy, consider some birth statistics from The Farm, a vegetarian community in Summertown, TN. During the years 1970 to 1989, 1,700 (mostly vegan) women at The Farm gave birth. Only 3 percent had any complications, and there were no maternal deaths. Making matters even better was an astonishingly low rate—only one in 1,700—of pre-eclampsia, a life-threatening condition prompted by malnutrition. Remember, these statistics were culled from women who, for the most part, ate *no animal products whatsoever.*

Another common worry is that a vegetarian diet can't provide the increased number of calories that a pregnant woman needs. The Recommended Dietary Allowances for a pregnant woman are 2,200 calories per day during the first trimester, 2,500 per day during the second trimester, and 2,800 per day during the third trimester. Experts disagree on how many calories a pregnant woman needs, making these guidelines merely what their name indicates—guidelines. For instance, due to morning sickness or other reasons, many pregnant women don't feel like eating much of anything during their first trimester, while some women feel hungry all the time. So rather than worrying about how many calories you're getting, focus on eating when you are hungry, particularly whole grains, fruits and vegetables. If you are eating a variety of foods, you will be giving both yourself and your baby the vitamin A, calcium, iron, and other nutrients that are needed for proper health and development. Remember to avoid junk foods and highly processed foods. They may be satisfying your urge to eat something, but they are doing little beyond that.

One caveat: If you are currently a pregnant meat eater, it is not the best time to change to a vegetarian diet. A pregnant woman's body is extremely sensitive and may have a difficult time handling dietary changes on top of the number of other changes that are occurring. A better idea is to gradually cut out meat before you get pregnant, so by the time baby is starting to develop, you've already handled the subtle switches the body undergoes when meat has been eliminated from the diet.

No Kidding—Veggie Youngsters Are Healthy and Happy

WORRIES ABOUT CHILDREN don't end with birth; some would say they begin there. Every parent frets over the food his or her child eats and how well that food is going to help the child to grow. These worries may be more pronounced with parents of vegetarian children, because some parents feel they are willfully omitting something from their children's diet that always has been recommended (and advertised) as health-promoting. Do kids need meat to be able to grow? No. Can they develop healthy teeth and bones without animal-derived calcium sources? Yes. Does a meatless diet provide enough protein and iron to *develop*, not merely *maintain*, healthy blood, immune systems, and muscles? Yes.

Through inborn parental instinct, you're probably skeptical when it comes to your children. That's a good trait. We'll answer some of your questions here, but when you are done reading this section, supplement this information by picking up one of the books we mention in the Further Reading section at the end of this chapter (page 169). Talk to other vegetarian parents to see what their worries were and how they were able to quell them. Notice how healthy and active their kids are in comparison to what you consider normal for the age.

For starters, we'd like to mention that the American Academy of Pediatrics and the American Dietetic Association have both published position papers that have vouched for the nutritional adequacy of vegetarian diets for children. Add to that the fact that for more than twenty years the National Academy of Sciences has supported giving a meatless diet to children, and you have three major players in the scientific world asserting that everything will be OK if you choose not to feed meat to your child. This may help calm your fears in a general way, but there are more specific questions about vegetarianism and kids, which in many cases mirror the concerns that adults voice when they decide to go veg.

Whether they are eleven months old or eleven years old, children need high-energy, nutrient-dense foods to support their rapidly growing bodies. You don't have much to worry about on the meat front for much of the first year, because breast milk or a full-fat, vitamin-enriched soy formula or milk formula will provide all the nutrients your child needs. (Do not use regular soymilk, just as you wouldn't use ordinary whole milk, because neither is formulated for infants.) When the child is ready to move on to solid foods, beans, grains, soyfoods, and vegetables (all high in nutrients including protein) can be ground up in the blender or chopped up and eaten as finger foods. Dairy products can be a good protein source, but deriving protein from vegetables helps avoid protein overload. It also keeps the body free from the hormones and antibiotics present in many dairy products. To make sure your child is getting enough calories, supplement his or her normal diet with nutrient-rich foods like avocados, nut butters, sweet potatoes, and dried fruits. By virtue of getting the proper amount of calories (provided it is coming from the right sources), you can make sure that protein needs are being fulfilled.

Dairy products also don't corner the market on being able to provide adequate calcium. Green, leafy vegetables like broccoli, kale, and spinach are all good sources, so are almonds and sesame seeds. Some kids don't relish the thought of a plateful of steaming kale staring them in the face, so calcium-fortified orange juice, fruit bars, calcium-fortified tofu, or calcium-fortified cereals are all viable alternatives. Mothers who are breast-feeding their infants need not worry about calcium. Babies get plenty of calcium from mother's milk, and studies show that this calcium is two to three times more absorbable than calcium from cow's milk. As for iron and vitamin C (which enhances iron absorption), kids can get enough of the recommended amounts from sources such as dried fruits, greens, legumes, and grains. Cooking these foods in cast-iron pots and pans increases the amount of absorbable iron even further.

This information may be good in theory, but what if you have one of the millions of children who won't eat their vegetables under any plea or threat? If the rest of their diet is anchored by fruits, beans, and grains and the veggies aren't being replaced by junk food, you will still be fulfilling nutritional requirements. You can also help matters by using a bit of ingenuity. Add vegetables to other foods that your child already likes, like sauces, breads, or potato dishes; cut the vegetables into fun shapes (a little sleight of hand never hurt anyone, right?); or let the child help you choose the family's vegetables when you're at the store.

Remember that a child's diet should not be dominated by sugar-laden foods or other "empty" calories (those that come from either sugars or fat and don't provide much nutritionally). And staying active and physically fit is just as important for your young child as it is for you. Regular exercise has shown to diminish the likelihood that a child will be obese, have high cholesterol, or develop hypertension. And if a child enjoys exercising when he or she is young, chances are that he or she will keep enjoying it right into adulthood. By teaching your children proper diet and exercise habits when they are young, you can make sure that they hit their teen years in full stride.

Surveying the Teen Scene

THE RULES OF GOOD NUTRITION don't change too much during the teen years, but the power dynamic certainly does. You probably have less say about what your child eats on a daily basis; you have to hope he or she has learned your lessons about good nutrition to sustain him or her for all those hours of the day that he or she's out of your sight.

Though you may not have raised your child as a vegetarian, there is an ever-increasing chance he or she may have already decided to make the switch to meatless before you've made your own commitment. Market research indicates that teenagers are the fastest growing segment of vegetarians in this country. It seems that more and more teens are reading about the harm a meat-based diet can do to both animals and the environment, and are using their own plate as a first means of protest. Some 80 percent say they are doing it to preserve the environment—not as a further attempt to drive their parents to the loony bin. It has become quite cool for teens to stand up for something, promote change, or try to make their community a better place to live. Young celebrities like Sara Gilbert of TV's "Roseanne" and the late River Phoenix have been well known for their outspoken support of vegetarianism, which has fueled the teen vegetarian craze. With their unfailing energy and raw passion, teens have shown that they have the drive and ability to be a cornerstone of the vegetarian movement in this country.

Worry is part of being the parent of a teenager, and parents of all teenagers worry about what their children are eating. If you have a teen who has recently declared an intention to go vegetarian, you may be worrying even more than normal. As with all issues that confront a teen, if parents harp on the topic too much, the teen will turn a deaf ear. Instead, teach by example; in this case, keep healthful, whole foods in the kitchen (bean burritos in the freezer, granola or whole grain cereals in the pantry, or juice instead of soft drinks in the refrigerator). Offer healthful dinners, and keep them simple, like pasta and sauce, tacos, homemade top-your-own pizza, and hearty salads with a variety of greens and vegetables in them. Above all, don't worry too much. Research published in *Adolescent Medicine* (October 1992) showed that vegetarian teens reportedly ate less junk food than their nonvegetarian friends.

The most common mistake a parent can make when his or her teen announces he or she is turning to a vegetarian diet is to put up barriers, to argue, or to belittle the decision as a fad, like clothes or a hairstyle. Our advice is to support the decision and get involved in it. Discuss the issues with your child and listen to why he or she is interested in becoming a vegetarian. Take opportunities to learn about it together. Work together on remaking the

Man's Best Meatless Friends?

VEGETARIAN PETS? It may sound like kind of a stretch right now, seeing that you're trying to get your own human diet in order. But there are some people who raise their dogs and cats on a meatless diet, and we didn't want to leave them out when talking about special groups. (Who knows if Fido or Kitty would have picked up this book when you were out and been offended by a potentially blatant omission?)

Raising your dog or cat as a vegetarian will get you raised eyebrows from many veterinarians, If you aren't going about it correctly, those raised eyebrows are in place for good reason. First, you need to know that even the Center for Veterinary Medicine, a division of the U.S. Food and Drug Administration, reports that many dog foods are made from the flesh of dead, dying, disabled, and diseased cattle. As long as this flesh is "properly" processed, it can be made into pet food. We as a society spend millions of dollars per year on vet care, and there are a growing number of vets

family's favorite recipes into meatless versions. Ask for advice or at least input on the weekly family menu. Learn about nutrition yourself and encourage a well-rounded meal, which could be simply adding a salad to pizza or lasagna, or adding a slice of whole wheat bread and a bowl of fruit salad for dessert. Always include your teen in the family's dinner plans, whether you plan to eat meat or not; if you're not enamored with cooking a separate vegetarian meal,

6

and researchers who say that we could avoid some of that expense and prolong the lives of our pets as we could our own by keeping this "dirty meat" away from them.

Your pets do have some tricky nutritional requirements that traditionally only meat is thought to provide. Cats need taurine (to prevent blindness), arachidonic acid (a fatty acid necessary to promote growth), and converted forms of vitamin A, while dogs need specially balanced amounts of calcium and vitamin D. To avoid meat-based products and still provide these nutrients, supplements must be added regularly and diligently. These supplements are now on the market as a result of years of research by a company called Harbingers of a New Age. Harbingers, based in Troy, Montana, ([406] 295-4944) has reported that its Vegedog, Vegecat, and Vegekit supplements have received glowing reports from 99 percent of the pet owners who have used them to supplement their pet's vegetarian diet. Enriched with vitamins, the supplements gain the aforementioned hard-to-find nutrients from previously untapped sources such as seaweed. Harbinger's supplies special recipes—made with vegan or vegetarian foods like rice, lentils, garbanzo beans, oats, nutritional yeast, carrots, and olive oil—to which the supplements are added.

Before starting your pet on any type of varied diet, you will want to consult a vet sympathetic to a vegetarian diet for pets and then do some other outside research to see if you believe vegetarianism is right for your animal. If we have the time and the inclination, chances are that many of our pets can do quite well without eating pet food of a questionable quality.

encourage your child to cook his or her own meal—or even prepare a meatless meal for the whole family—and then lend a hand if it is needed. This strategy is a good way to keep everyone involved and also teaches your teen some valuable cooking lessons so he or she can be independent when heading off into the real world.

When it comes to the decision to stop eating meat, the only time you should worry is if your teen shows signs of an eating disorder. If your teen is only eating nonfat yogurt and drinking water, you know you have a real problem, and it has nothing to do with vegetarianism. Otherwise, what your teen really needs is support. The fact that you or other members of your family aren't yet vegetarian doesn't really matter. Take it to heart that your teen is trying to do something for him- or herself and the world.

If you're still concerned about whether your child is getting enough nutrients, you need only to re-read the section on vegetarian children; the nutrition advice hasn't changed. You will need to monitor the typical teenager's tendency to snack constantly and eat a lot of junk food, however. No matter if your teen is a meat-eater or a vegetarian, he or she shouldn't be subsisting on Twinkies and diet soda. You also need to lend a sensitive ear to other problems that your veg teen may encounter, such as a lack of choices in the school cafeteria, or peer pressure from friends or parents of friends who don't understand (see the next section for more details on this situation). If you can establish a supportive, trusting relationship with your vegetarian teen, you may find after a while that he or she is teaching you a thing or two about good eating habits.

When You're Away from Home

THE SHOPPING, PLANNING, and preparation of vegetarian meals we discussed in Chapter 3 (pages 47–112) is a great idea—when you're at home to do it. But you know that depending on your schedule you eat some meals away from home. If you travel, have business lunches out with clients, or dine with friends, there are times that your vegetarian needs may not take top billing. Here are some handy tips that will aid you in maintaining your vegetarianism no matter where you are.

Travel

More and more Americans are spending their work week hurriedly hopping planes, trains, and automobiles. If you are part of this group, you may wonder how you can possibly stay vegetarian when you barely have a moment to think about what you're eating in the first place. And airline and train food is for the most part notoriously inedible at worst and passable at best. We don't want to discourage you, but it's likely that no amount of planning will guarantee a vegetarian meal, let alone a tasty one. This is not to say that there is nothing you can do to make your situation better. Your first and safest option is to eat before you embark or to take some food with you. However, there are things you can do to ensure that you get a vegetarian meal on the plane you're on. Whether it is of acceptable quality will vary from airline to airline.

Request a vegetarian meal when you make your reservations, and make sure that some acknowledgment of your meal choice appears on your printed itinerary when you receive it. When you check in at the ticket counter, you may want to check again with the ticket agent that the meal request has been logged and honored; that way, if there has been a mix-up, there is a chance there can be one last-ditch effort to take care of things before you're 30,000 feet in the air.

When you board your flight, remind the flight attendant of your special meal request. If you decide to move seats, tell someone so that your meal is not given to someone else or misplaced. Then sit back, relax, and wait to see what is delivered. Airlines are improving their vegetarian selections, but the bottom line is, you just never know whether you're going to get a tasty curry with rice or a lump of oatmeal and a stalk of broccoli, an actual vegetarian offering on one airline.

When you're off the plane and at the hotel, your options expand by leaps and bounds. If the hotel has a restaurant or two, you can usually call to see if they have vegetarian options or if they would create one for you—a meatless pasta, for example, or a baked potato with toppings. If you're unfamiliar with the restaurants surrounding your hotel, ask the hotel concierge to give you a list of restaurants in the area. Many hotels have a current list that is organized by category, even including vegetarian. If all this fails, you can usually find a pizza joint nearby for a cheese pie with various vegetables or a fast-food establishment with a salad bar. It's not gourmet, but it's better than going hungry.

Business Lunches

When you're out with clients, the last thing you want is for your dietary choices to dominate the discussion. And you don't want to make a scene at a steakhouse when everyone is downing a sirloin and you've ordered a baked potato and a tossed salad. In order to avoid these potentially distracting situations so you can get down to business, take just a little time to prepare before the big event.

There are many ways you can circumvent the vegetarian issue before it ever becomes an issue. First, try to be the member of the group who decides where to meet. If you don't have that control, suggest an ethnic restaurant. Italian, Chinese, Indian, and Ethiopian restaurants are all well known for their variety of tasty vegetable dishes; at these establishments, you can choose a pasta or vegetable dish without anyone taking notice. If you're trying someplace new and aren't familiar with the menu, call ahead to see if the restaurant has a variety of vegetarian options. Another possibility is to suggest a vegetarian restaurant. Many businesspeople are so used to being taken to the same old places that they can't wait to try something new.

The most important point to make regarding situations like this is not to let them dominate you or your preparation for a big meeting. You may feel that it's best to simply get the whole vegetarian issue out of the way immediately, and move on to other things. If your vegetarianism and the questions that inevitably accompany it come up, so be it. You know you're fully prepared to answer them based on your reading of Chapter 2 (pages 15–45). Answer them gracefully and get back on your way to closing that big deal.

You may find yourself having your biggest difficulties at an awards dinner or special luncheon where the rubberized Chicken-You-Name-It is the standard fare. When you R.S.V.P., announce that you are vegetarian and ask that a meatless meal be prepared for you. That way you can get your meal at the same time as everyone else and not cause a scene. If that's not possible, you might have to grin and bear it with the good old salad and baked potato. After the function is over, take yourself out for a special vegetarian treat.

Dining at a Friend's or Relative's House

If you have guests coming over to your house, you'll have no trouble impressing them with the variety and taste of vegetarian food. Be it a Mexican fiesta, do-it-yourself-pizzas, or tangy marinated-and-grilled vegetables, your dinner parties are sure to be a hit, and probably a little out of the ordinary for most people. But when you're not on your home turf, you generally have little influence over what is served. Many new vegetarians feel guilty when heading over to the home of a friend who has slaved all day over that new beef recipe, only to find out that his or her guests don't eat beef.

Close friends or relatives probably know that you've made the switch to a vegetarian diet. When discussing it with them, don't treat it lightly. Ask for their support, and show them that this isn't just some passing fancy. Being knowledgeable about the subject is one of the best ways to show that you've done your homework. If they know in advance that vegetarianism is something you're serious about, they are more likely to respect your eating habits and cook something that everyone can eat or at least have enough side dishes available for you to sample.

> When invited to a friend's or relative's for dinner, rather than ask them to make something special for you, offer to bring a course or side dish. Chances are, everyone will enjoy trying something new and different, and you'll be sure to have something to eat!

If you are faced with steak as the main course, do your best to avoid it gracefully. Eat the side dishes, and don't make a big deal out of the fact that you've chosen to forgo the meat. If you don't make it look like you're offended, there is less of a chance that your hosts may take offense. They may ask why you're only eating salad, corn on the cob, and a baked potato, and then you can gently tell or remind them. Then, your needs will be considered at future dinner parties.

When the Road Gets Rocky

TO HELP YOU CIRCUMVENT some potentially sticky situations, we've provided some of advice. To help you get over some of the misconceptions that are commonly held about vegetarianism, we've presented the facts. But we're smart enough to know that for some, the switch to vegetarianism can be a difficult one. There can be nagging doubts that are difficult to shake. There are friends who won't be so understanding when you turn down their favorite pork chop dish. There are business lunches where you've made the appropriate arrangements, and you still wind up paying $20 for a plate of soggy vegetables.

For some new vegetarians, these uncomfortable feelings can be enough to make them wonder why they ever wanted to make the switch in the first place. One individual was asked in a *Vegetarian Times* interview why he started eating animal products again, even though he knew that a vegetarian diet was best for him. He was blunt about it. "Where I fall back is when I want to socialize with the rest of the world," he said. "It takes a lot of energy to eat differently from most of society." You, too, may find that being a vegetarian at home is much easier than when you are faced with the rest of the meat-eating world.

Your first goal when choosing vegetarianism is to choose it for yourself and to work on your own values and goals. If you live in a family where your spouse is a meat eater and has no intention of becoming a vegetarian, don't preach and prod. Do your best to respect everyone's diet choices, and they in turn may learn to respect yours. A much better way to show people that you're not off your rocker is to share your best-tasting vegetarian dishes with them and do all you can to stay healthy. If you do both, who can question your judgment? Many meat eaters will feel pressured when a family member becomes a vegetarian. They may think that someone (you) will be judging them at every meal and telling them how they're going to die as a result of what they're eating. If you keep these acrimonious situations well away from your dinner table, peace and harmony will prevail.

It is important to note that eating meat has been ingrained in our culture for many years and that many more Americans are meat eaters than not. Meat eating is a symbol of affluence. It is the centerpiece of many a family gathering. And many people are so used to either preparing and eating meat for holidays that they could not imagine the holiday without it. When you become a vegetarian, you are going against tradition, culture, and familiarity. For some, these odds seem too difficult to overcome. For others, they are minor bumps on the road to a happier, healthier life. Simply knowing that there will be hurdles on your road to vegetarianism is a good way to avoid them. If you stop eating meat under the assumption that it will be a breeze, you may be less prepared for any problems that may arise. If you are well schooled in the answers, you can role-play a bad situation in your mind into a good one. When the real situation comes up, just put your knowledge into active practice.

Logistical problems, such as living in a remote location that isn't exactly a health-food mecca, are no cause for despair. A state or local vegetarian society can be a great source of information. You can find out what society is closest to you by writing the Vegetarian Resource Group, P.O. Box 1463, Baltimore, MD 21203; (410) 366-VEGE. A vegetarian society can lend suggestions regarding finding the names of co-ops or companies from which you can order natural food.

Your computer can be a great tool. There are several on-line billboards or forums on the Internet, CompuServe, America Online, and others that vegetarians frequent. By merely posting a message in one of these forums explaining your predicament, you can exchange recipes or get advice from vegetarians across the country who have probably experienced your same troubles at one time or another. In addition, keep reading to expand your knowledge about diet, nutrition, disease, the environment, and animal rights. Be a scholar of your plate, never accepting what you've learned as enough. Some people will have a tremendous struggle, while others can wake up one day and vow never to eat meat again. If you slip up, don't give up. You're in the process of change, and there is always room for a little human error.

Mothers have always been told to give their children milk; that won't change anytime soon. And most teenagers will go through their lives learning to eat cheeseburgers if they want to get big and strong. People will eat meat around you whether you're a vegetarian or not. These are all facts of life that neither this book nor any amount of teaching will be able to change in the short term. But to be honest, these realities should mean little. You are at a point where you are trying to revamp your own thoughts on proper eating and living. It is pointless to try to influence what other people do. You are more likely to influence others when you put up your own life as an example.

Go Greenly into That Great Night

WELL, BEGINNING VEGETARIAN, our short time with you is just about over. We set out at the start of this book to teach you a little about a meatless diet and hope that we have answered some of your questions. And like we said at the end of the first chapter, the choice is yours. Whether you choose to use what you've learned about diet and nutrition as a springboard to reduce the amount of meat you eat or eliminate it completely is your own personal choice. But we encourage you to use the recipe section when you want some quick and easy vegetarian recipes and to refer back to some of what you've read when you need a little information refresher.

The attitude toward vegetarianism in the past two decades has undergone a dramatic change. When it comes right down to it, being a vegetarian is about good health, good food, and goodwill toward all beings that walk the Earth. Beyond that, it becomes whatever you want it to be.

When an old movie or television show would end, they would fade to black. We prefer to fade to green. And we're pretty sure by now you understand why.

Further Reading

Pregnancy, Children and the Vegan Diet, by Michael Klaper, M.D. (Gentle World Inc., 1987).

Vegetarian Children, by Sharon Yntema (McBooks Press, 1987).

The Vegetarian Mother Baby Book, by Rose Elliot (Pantheon Books, 1986).

Vegetarian Pregnancy, by Sharon Yntema (McBooks Press, 1994).

Index

Z

If you've enjoyed

READING and COOKING from ─────────┐

Vegetarian Times Vegetarian Beginner's Guide,

┌───────────── you'll love

❀ Vegetarian Times Complete Cookbook,

This best-selling cookbook is the new bible
on the vegetarian lifestyle.
It includes:

❀ More than 600 recipes

❀ Dozens of vegetarian menus

❀ A glossary of vegetarian ingredients

❀ Information on the health benefits
of a vegetarian diet

❀ Explanations of cooking techniques

❀ Shopping lists for stocking
the vegetarian pantry

And much, much
more

Macmillan • USA
ISBN 0-02-621745-7
$29.95
Available in bookstores everywhere

Vegetarian Times
Complete Cookbook
by the Editors of Vegetarian Times

More than 600 Delicious and
Healthful Meatless Dishes plus:

How to plan a healthy vegetarian diet

Cooking techniques for maximum flavor and nutrition

Dozens of vegetarian menus

A glossary of vegetarian ingredients

And much more